Kayak Across France

Kayak Across France

A Canal and River Adventure Unlocked

Nigel Foster

NIGEL
KAYAKS

NIGEL
KAYAKS

Library of Congress Control Number: 2021917062
ISBN: 978-1-7364203-1-7 (paperback)
ASIN: B09DC1H1S8 (Kindle)

Design by Nigel Foster.
Cover photographs by Kristin Nelson and Nigel Foster.
Maps by Nigel Foster.
All photos courtesy of Kristin Nelson and Nigel Foster.
Printed by Amazon.

Publisher Nigel Kayaks
www.nigelkayaks.com

To my wife, Kristin.

Contents

List of Maps

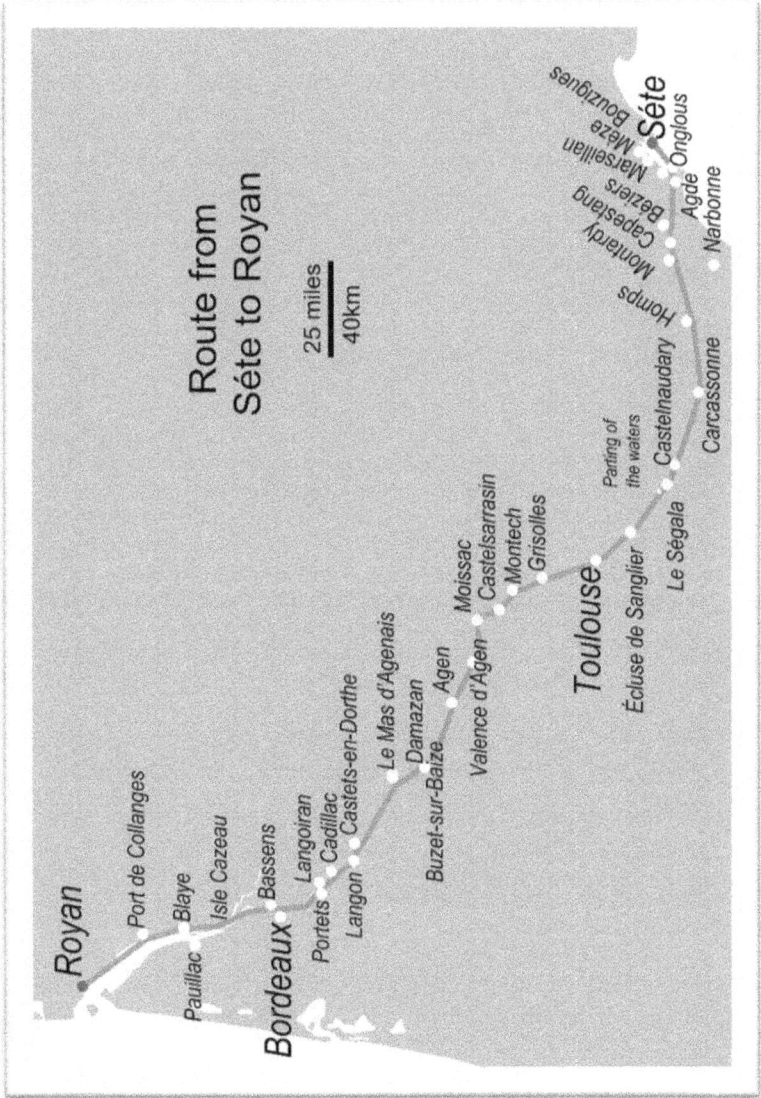

MAP 1. Route from Sète to Royan

ix

1. Head for the Sun

Your broad brimmed hat
And a glass of wine
For an azure dream of summertime. [1]

Tim Franklin slammed the front door from the rain, his mop of dense curly black hair gleaming, moisture dripping from the ends. "Hi Nige!" he greeted me cheerfully. "Do you want to go somewhere warm this winter? Sunshine, wine, beaches?" Here, in Sussex, England, our winter was already cold, wet, and windy.

We both ran outdoor programs at different residential centers. My winter outdoor schedule was teaching environmental subjects, to eleven-year-old children. Combining my vacation time, which ran annually from April 1st, with days off in lieu of weekends, I had four weeks of leave due. As if a cruel April Fool's joke, I could not carry over any of my annual vacation time past the end of March. Tim's situation was similar. We both had a good slice of time available, but at an inconvenient time of year.

My dreams lay far to the north, where summer daylight lingers throughout the night. The summer before, Tim and I cut our sea kayaks in half to fly them to Newfoundland. Descending the river from Gander Lake, we explored the Atlantic coast. Labrador now attracted me, but that kind of trip had little appeal in winter.

Tim peeled off his jacket, shedding a few pints of rainwater in hanging it up. He was killing time to best effect and held my full attention by the time he turned to elaborate.

"I took out a library book about French canals," he began enthusiastically. "You can get all the way from Calais to the Mediterranean by canal. We could go by kayak, zip down to spend a few days on the beach and then paddle back." He paused, trying to gauge my reaction. "It's only seven hundred kilometers! Just think, we would only need to average about twenty-four kilometers a day: fifteen miles. That's nothing!"

I readily agreed to the plan, but as the Scottish poet Robert Burns wrote in 1785:

> *In proving foresight may be vain:*
> *The best-laid schemes o' mice an' men,*
> *Gang aft agley,*
> *An' lea'e us nought but grief an' pain,*
> *For promis'd joy.*[2]

Another way of putting it might be, *if it sounds too good to be true, it probably is*. Over the following days and weeks of planning, troubling details began to trickle in like rainwater dribbling down the back of my neck, little by little. For instance: a mere detail of oversight, but seven hundred kilometers would get us to the Med' but not back.

"No matter," Tim pointed out. "It's all flat water. If we use a tandem kayak, we will fly along! Forty-eight kilometers a day is still doable. Thirty miles? Easy!"

But then he discovered that the distances in his French canal book were imperial, not metric. It would not be fourteen hundred kilometers, but fourteen hundred miles. Could we average forty-five miles a day over a whole month? Extremely doubtful.

At *The Bell*, our local village inn, one evening soon after, we warmed ourselves as close to the log fire as we could get. Then we clacked our brimming glasses of foamy Guinness together. "Cheers!"

As I raised my glass to my lips, I noticed Tim was watching me too closely, his own glass lowered. He waited till I sipped before delivering the coup de grace: "Two hundred and twenty locks."

I exhaled. Guinness foam flew. As I choked, Tim casually added with a smirk: "That's each way." His timing, as always, was impeccable.

Forty-five miles, plus fourteen locks, every day? No! Nevertheless we continued to plan. Our route would start at Calais and run close to the Belgian border. We would climb up the Marne valley, through the middle of Champagne wine country, and then descend the Saône and Rhône to the Mediterranean. On the Marne canal, said Tim, women controlled most of the locks.

What about paddling back? We would figure that out later if we got that far. We borrowed a red tandem kayak, a *Tasman* from Kirton Kayaks, which we lovingly referred to as the *Baguette Rouge*. Modifying it where necessary to accommodate our unavoidable deck cargo, we also built a trolly for portages.

Having little time to spare, we had only one opportunity to paddle the kayak, for a quick sprint lasting one hour during a wintery shower. As we climbed out, crisp with ice, we hoped it would be warmer in France the following week. It simply remained for us to pack our bags and catch the late-night ferry from Dover after work.

The first of March? France? What were we thinking? I sat up. The white shape beside me was Tim, his sleeping bag coated in frost. Beside us on the stone quay at Calais, where we lay in the open to sleep, stood the glittering shapes of our kayak and bags. Having arrived in the dead of night, I saw now in the faint light of morning how everything appeared sparkly. All, that is, except for the dark metal hulks of the ships moored nearby, the cranes poised at the ready, and the prospect of getting out of my warm cocoon.

I nudged Tim awake with my foot so he could appreciate the moment too.

How many locks? "Two hundred and twenty…each way?"

Following the frozen canals of the first days came incessant rain that flooded the valleys. Neither ice nor flood was really a surprise, nor was the snow. We forged on, driven by the vision of a sunny beach and a broad horizon of azure sea.

In the years that followed, Tim's canal book, that is, my purchased copy, not the one he borrowed from the library, took its place alongside others of its kind: those about the dark arts. I considered binding it with steel bands and powerful curses lest anyone, especially me, should succumb to the temptation of the Sirens' call.

More rain.

But it did not have to be that way. One of the routes described in it followed an ancient canal, the Canal du Midi, which crosses from the Mediterranean to Toulouse. Another connects onward to the Atlantic. How would that be in summer, cruising through the famous wine regions of France? I saw myself relaxing at a café sipping early morning coffee, and food shopping at summer markets. The idea, with others, lay dormant. More than forty years passed before the right opportunity presented itself.

Why explore wine country alone? Lured by my idea was Seattle ceramic artist, and seasoned kayaker, Kristin Nelson. Lean, athletic and abundantly cheerful, Kristin has a quirky personality that is full of surprises. She once issued a stern warning to a polar bear sniffing her kayak within paw-swipe of her, demanding, "Bear! Be Gone!"[3] Did it leave? You bet!

Frosty morning on the route south.

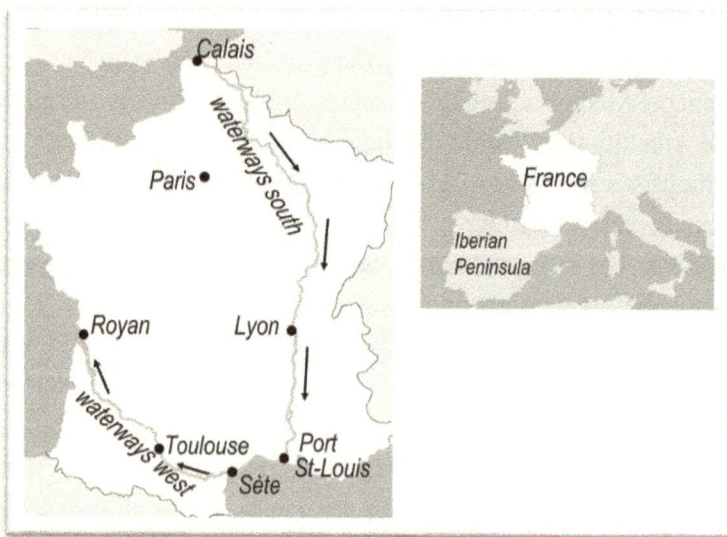

MAP 2. Canal and River Routes across France.

2. Sète and Match

One day, into the Ocean
(I no longer know beneath which skies)
I threw an offering to nothing,
Quite a little precious wine...[4]

Our colorful convoy left the pebble beach beside a yacht club and floated onto the calm of Étang de Thau. Located sixty miles west of Port-Saint-Louis-du-Rhône, Étang de Thau is a saltwater lagoon. It parallels the Mediterranean shore, stretching northeast and southwest, ten miles long and two to three miles wide. A narrow bar, just half a mile wide, separates it from the sea: a bar fringed with sandy Mediterranean beaches on one side, sagging into marshes along the étang shore on the other. There, in the shallow edge of the lagoon, seahorses cling to seagrasses, and pink flamingos tuck their heads to their feet to feed.

Patrick confidently led the way, paddling one of the three tandems. Short, stocky and dark-haired, he runs a kayak instruction and guiding business, kayakmed.com, here on the Mediterranean coast. Élouise, his young daughter, sat relaxing in the front seat of his kayak, her neat braid of thick hair hanging from beneath her big white cap.

In the other kayaks, Martine, Patrick's wife, teamed up with her friend Madeleine, their sunglasses and caps shielding the sun, while Kristin joined me. We would paddle clockwise around the island of Sète, a near-circular limestone hill that stands above an otherwise low coastline.

From the hilltop, the coastal views are panoramic. Few other coastal places stand high between the Rhône and the Pyrenees. Built as the Mediterranean port for the then-proposed Canal du Midi, Sète continues to be an important port despite the decline in trade along the Canal du Midi. I considered this the perfect place to begin our trip across France. But first, for symbolic purposes, it seemed fitting to paddle out onto the Mediterranean before heading inland, across Languedoc,

"Come look over here!" Patrick called, as he showed the way through a narrow channel. This detour, he explained, was to see the small fishing boats where a shantytown of little fishing huts lined the shore. Short jetties with makeshift huts spidered over the water, small open boats beside. Nets hung to air amid stacks of baskets and piles of wooden poles. A breeze twisted the fingers of a ragged French flag.

"The fishermen catch daurade when they swim between the pond and the sea." *The pond,* Patrick referred to, was the Étang de Thau. *Daurade* was the delicious fish he cooked for our arrival, sea bream.

"They often use nets, sometimes lines, but when the daurade come through in a big school, many fish swim tightly together! Everyone goes crazy and all the nets and lines get into a big tangle. People get angry and shout!" His face expressed joy at the recollected mayhem.

We doubled back into the main channel to see where the fish would pass, and where the tangle occurred. There, from beneath a bridge, we emerged onto the street-like canals of Sète, a stately area like a mini-Venice. Here to either side of the broad canal, a wall of pale-painted houses stood shoulder to shoulder, variously two, four, or three storeys high, like uneven teeth. The buildings stared from beneath shallow-pitched roofs of orange clay pantiles, across quays against which small boats had moored.

Several open boats, brightly painted in either red and white, or blue and white, each had a strange stern-mounted structure. This consisted of a ramp of steps climbing back above the water to a small high platform.

"What are those for," I asked, wondering if an observer might stand up high to spy fish.

Jousting boats at Sète.

"Jousting boats," said Patrick. "The men stand up at the top carrying a lance and a wooden shield, while ten rowers on each boat race the two boats past each other. The two jousters try to dislodge each other from the little platforms behind. When one succeeds, the vanquished knight tumbles into the canal.

"The men are big! And strong!" Patrick puffed out his chest and beat it. "Some are one hundred and eighty kilos big," (four hundred pounds). He laughed. "They make a great splash!"

"It is a tradition here since 1666, when they built Sète. Like knights on horses, but on boats instead." Could we watch? Not this time: September was too late in the year. We had missed the final tournament by just shy of two weeks.

Jousting on boats seemed such a bizarre activity. What inspired it? Did it start while it was common for men to joust on horseback? In France, horseback jousting declined after a splinter of lance stabbed the French King Henry II in the eye during a tournament. He died later of sepsis from his eye wound, and from brain damage. That was in 1559, more than a century before the founding of Sète.

So, had fishermen in the Mediterranean continued jousting ever since those times? The first documented record of water jousting in France was as early as 1177, in Lyon, so in likelihood it simply survived while horseback jousting did not.

We continued along the main canal, between grand buildings, until we came to large fishing boats tied up to docks.

"Tuna boats," Patrick pointed out disapprovingly. "They are ruthless. They chase even the last fish! Soon there will be none, the boat owners are so greedy. They make so much money they can buy the best equipment to find the tuna, and the best gear to catch them all." He shook his head sadly.

"Are there not quotas?" I asked.

"Yes, but some owners register their boats in Tunis to get around the quotas. See how that one has its name in Arabic script? Registered in Tunis, they are not subject to European quotas, but this is still their base. They bring more tuna in here than to anywhere else in the world.

"But that's not all that's bad here," he continued with a frown. "Over that side," he pointed toward to the docks to the east, "they import exotic hardwoods. Greenpeace is not happy."

From the canal, we entered the wider harbor entrance and aimed toward a long, detached, stone breakwater that offered shelter. There our kayaks slid to a halt, side by side on the sand beach at its base.

"We will stop here for some lunch," Patrick announced happily as we brought our kayaks ashore. "No need to carry them farther," he assured me, shaking his head. Noting my hesitation, and rightly guessing the reason, he added, "There is almost no tide here. Just a few centimeters."

I followed him up to the white stonework and turned, gazing out at the brightness of the town on the hill. Sailboats slid quietly past. Anglers cast their lines, while a few topless sunbathers cooled their feet at the edge of the cerulean blue water.

Patrick, settling on the wall, poured a little sweet wine from a thermos and opened a plastic container. He had tuna, tomato, and onion. Tuna from here? I did not ask. Having also unwrapped bread and cheese, he invited us to eat, and drink.

This breakwater offered two entrances to the harbor, one sometimes more sheltered than the other.

"Over there," he pointed, "where the buildings are, was a quarantine where people would stay for forty days if they arrived ill, before being offered the freedom of Sète."

Before getting afloat again, we switched positions in our kayaks. Martine joined me, and Kristin went with Madeleine. Leaving the harbor for the Mediterranean, we came to low limestone cliffs with caves we stopped to explore. Seen from the teal-colored water, within the cool of the caves, the sunlight glowed through the water as fluorescent turquoise. The sea felt alive, but the joyful energy of waves was short-lived. We soon entered another canal, looping back around the other side of the hill toward Étang de Thau again. There in the water fluttered a strange dark bat-like creature. Just a few inches long, it hovered close beneath the surface using a weird rippling motion. Its mesmerizing dance captivated me, but what was this dancer?

"A *lièvre de mer*," Patrick explained.

"What?" I asked. "What is one of those?"

"A rabbit?" Patrick tried to explain. "A big one, what do you call that? Big ears."

"A jackrabbit?" guessed Kristin.

"Okay, a sea jackrabbit," agreed Patrick uncertainly.

"A hare?" I ventured. I did not know what a jackrabbit was. Patrick preferred jackrabbit to hare. But neither sea hare nor sea jackrabbit made any sense to me.

We watched it for a little longer as it flapped around going nowhere. We found the animal later in one of Élousise's books. It was *Aplysia fasciata*. This shell-less gastropod feeds on algae in shallow water. It evades capture by deploying a squid-like ink cloud, and a diversionary secretion, into the water. A predator mistakes the secretion for the presence of food, allowing the sea hare to escape.

Approaching Étang de Thau.

"Sète is almost an island," Patrick admitted when we reached a dead end. "They blocked the channel when building the road. We have to climb."

That proved awkward, with our cumbersome tandems. But one at a time we hauled them up the wall, over the barrier fence and across the road. From there, we lifted over another fence to drop each kayak to the water, finally climbing down aboard.

Soon, we passed a fortification and reentered the Étang de Thau beside a long breakwater. Turning toward where we began our trip, we at once grounded in shallows. Reluctantly, we detoured far from shore alongside the breakwater in search of deep enough water.

The light was already fading into evening. Tomorrow Kristin and I would set off on our journey toward the Atlantic.

I remembered the 1979 trip with Tim. It took us three of our four available weeks to cover half of the distance between Calais and the Mediterranean. At that point, the canal led us through a tunnel from the north-draining Marne valley, to the Saône, which ran south. The Saône joined the Rhône at Lyon, carrying us swiftly to Port-Saint-Louis-du-Rhône and the Mediterranean.

This time, Kristin and I flew from Seattle to Paris. We met Richard Öhman, owner of Point65 Sweden, at a convenient place near the airport. Driving from home in France on his way to Sweden, Richard carried a tandem kayak on his roof rack for us to use. The model, *DoubleShot,* manufactured by Point65 Sweden, was of my own design.

We attached Richard's roof rack to our rental car and strapped the kayak on top. Over a quick coffee and breakfast, we caught up on news from Richard and his wife Camilla before they hurried north. We turned south.

Soon our route to Sète ran beside the rivers I kayaked with Tim. I tried to recognize the view from the motorway as I recalled seeing it from the river. I would not describe the drive from Lyon, alongside the River Rhône, as scenic: the view had been better from the water. The river had impressed me before, seen in flood from a kayak, so I was disappointed at how little I could see of it from the car. Yet I still felt a thrill of excitement: a little feeling of déjà vu.

The long flight and long drive had exhausted us by the time Patrick met us in the dark. He led us up the hill in Sète to meet Martine, and to welcome us into their home. Patrick served us a wonderful meal of locally caught Daurade, and fish pie.

We were happy to have a couple of days in which to prepare for our trip, and to see Sète. Patrick kept his kayaks at a farm along the coast some six miles to the southwest, on the narrow coastal strip between l'Étang de Thau and the Mediterranean. There we collected two tandems in readiness for our trip around Sète, and then went to view *the pond* from its marshy edge.

Strange plywood boxes littered the muddy shore. Some resembled the cab and hood of an old Land Rover pickup, but with neither wheels nor bed. Boxy. They were windowless as such, but instead of a windshield, a hinged flap lifted to offer a forward view from inside. What were these?

Patrick laughed. "They are for duck hunting," he said. "The ducks fly across the Mediterranean from Africa without stopping. They arrive tired and come down to shelter here. The hunters tether live ducks on the water; decoys to make it look a safe place to rest. Hunters call them *Judas ducks*. Then, Bam!"

"Don't they use wooden ducks?" I asked, visualizing wooden decoys.

"I don't know these wood ducks. Are they real?" he asked. "Do they hunt them with a wooden gun?"

3. Étang de Thau

The time has come, the Walrus said,
To talk of many things:
Of shoes, and ships, and sealing-wax,
Of cabbages and kings
And why the sea is boiling hot,
And whether pigs have wings.[5]

And now, the Walrus sat down to eat his meal. To it he added a little salt and vinegar, and bread and butter. Lewis Carroll's little oysters, invited to leave their bed for a walk along the beach, began to regret their eagerness. Too late, they realized the walrus had invited them to a meal of which they would be the main part.

Meanwhile, in our kayak laden with camping equipment, we crossed Étang de Thau directly into a stiff breeze that kicked up an urgent chop. Our bow, lurching forward; split the little breakers. Briny spray, flung into our faces, hazed our sunglasses. Our target lay a short distance north of the ancient town, Mèze, on the far shore. But before we came close, we ran into metal frames that stood four or five feet out of the water. Rows of these frames stretched for more than two miles between Mèze, and neighboring Bouzigues, covering the lagoon from shore to a mile out. These were oyster farms.

The metal frames, reaching up from the bed of the lagoon, stood separated by corridors for boat access. Each block, or so it appeared, consisted of a group of sixteen frames, in a double row of eight. The French government rent the plots to fishermen, who glue oysters onto the ropes that hang into the water from the frames. They also keep oysters in net bags, hanging them above water at times to mimic a low tide. The annual harvest from Étang de Thau is as much as thirteen thousand tons, enough for more than a few walruses and carpenters.

Étang de Thau oyster frames.

We made our way between the frames all the way to shore, hoping to find shelter there from the offshore wind. Then we hugged the land past the small buildings used by the oyster farmers. An open metal frame structure, to hoist and suspend a small work boat above the waves, stood in the water in front of each building. A conveyor belt for the shellfish led ashore toward stacks of colorful plastic crates.

The farmers market most of the oysters grown here as *huîtres de Bouzigues,* after the town Bouzigues. They are widely known, since Mèze and Bouzigues together constitute the largest shellfish farming area in the Mediterranean.

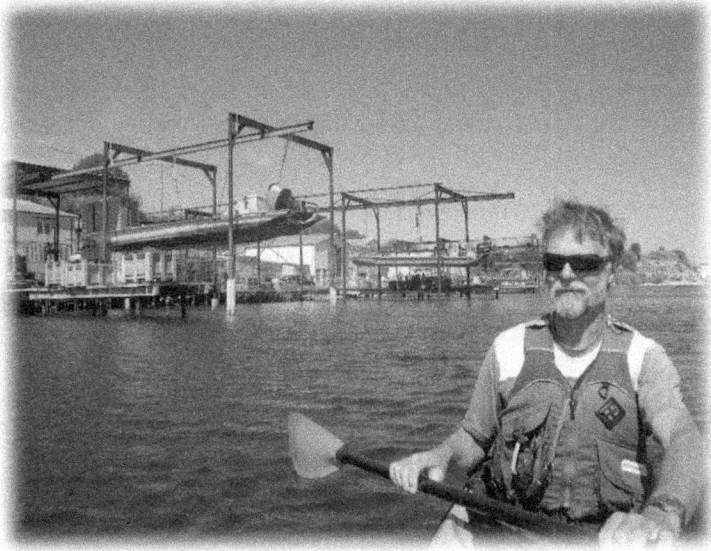

Oyster businesses near Mèze.

The old town of Mèze was important as a Phoenician port, at a time when the Mediterranean coastal geography was a little different. Then, a string of lagoons, including the Étang de Thau, connected all the way from the Rhône to the Pyrenees. They created a continuous sheltered waterway, used for transport and trade.

More recently, in 118 BC, the Romans built their first road in Gaul. This, the Via Domitia, ran from Italy to the Iberian Peninsula, (now Spain and Portugal). Mèze, as a port of call, was no doubt important even then for shellfish and wine.

The fish houses and jetties along the shore, with their offshore shellfish frames, now stretch all the way to Marseillan. A port since Phoenician times around 600 BC, Marseillan is one of the oldest towns in France. It is another of the towns via which the Romans directed the road, Via Domitia.

From the water, the most obvious features of Marseillan are the long harbor arms that protect the two marinas, yet a commercial dock extends directly inland between broad quays. It is there that the Noilly Prat company has quay frontage, warehouses, and a large open-air yard. In the yard, vermouth is aged for a year, in oak casks sprayed with water. This is la Maison Noilly Prat.

Noilly Prat has made vermouth here since the mid- nineteenth century. But the business began earlier when Joseph Noilly opened a grocery, and then a wine and spirit business, near Lyon, in 1813. He started his vermouth production there. It was a convenient location, since wormwood, and some of the other ingredients he used for flavoring, came from the mountains around Lyon.

Joseph's son, Louis, with Louis's son-in-law, Claude Prat, set up the new facility here in Marseillan. Aware how the color and flavor of fortified wines improved when transported on long ocean voyages; they simulated the shipping conditions while aging their vermouth at Marseillan.

Lewis Carroll's Walrus and Carpenter added a dash of vinegar to their oysters. Here it is customary to use dry vermouth instead: Noilly Prat.

From Marseillan we could see the white lighthouse with a red cap, the Phare des Onglous, which marks the entrance to the Canal du Midi. Across from the lighthouse stood a shorter green starboard marker. We worked across the last, exposed, stretch of l'Étang de Thau to enter the canal.

The windswept mouth of the canal seemed forlorn. Boats, including a long commercial barge, clung to the left bank, or sat moored at the quay beside the official canal buildings.

Étang de Thau

Entering the Canal du Midi.

Here were a few sailboats, with rigging rattling against masts too tall for the canal bridges. A few motorboats wallowed between them, some sinking, some sunk at their moorings. Had each of these fulfilled someone's travel dreams on the Canal du Midi? Had their owners intended to return? I felt sad to see boats so neglected, so abandoned.

Smoke filled the air ahead. The land to the east of the canal was on fire. Flames waved high, amid smoke that twisted in the wind and clung to the trees. Wailing sirens heralded the arrival of fire trucks; the sound drawing people to the opposite shore to watch. Reluctant to push through the thick, white, smoke, we landed to join the gathering crowd.

Once the grass fire was under control, we were able to pass. Overgrown grassy banks now hid the southernmost, and shallowest, corner of the Étang de Thau. The canal cuts across this shallow corner. Two miles farther on we spied a gap, and paddled through it, entering a narrow waterway which branched at once. Hidden from sight at the junction, we stopped and climbed onto an old bridge. There, sheltered from the breeze, on the sun-warmed concrete, we found a comfortable place to sit for lunch.

"That is the Grand Bagnas," I pointed across to where a marsh-fringed pond stretched green and shallow. Les étangs du Bagnas are two ponds, the smaller of which dries in summer. Together, they are a national nature reserve. Were they once part of Étang de Thau? If not, they must have connected to it. The reeds in the nearest corner, secluded, rang with bird song. Here, and there, fish popped the ripple-frosted water. A fat water vole swam slowly along the edge, floating high, with chestnut fur, and whiskers gleaming. It ducked out of sight beneath the overhang of vegetation.

From the horizon, a straight ribbon of reflected sky ran toward our feet, where a rusted sluice stood half raised. Long, dry, grasses overflowed the banks on either side of the blue ribbon. A few hundred yards away, a clump of tufted bushes and a tree grew beside a derelict house. Time and weather had stripped the roof off the building to a few bones of timber. Each dark window framed a void with no pane. Nothing could hinder the exploring fingers of the breeze.

Turning at the sound of a motor behind us, we watched a Pénichette, a French-designed boat built following the lines of a traditional French barge, pass slowly along the canal. *Campignol,* I read on its nameplate. We would follow in the same direction.

Étang de Thau

Water vole.

Our repast was simple and fresh: slices of apple, salami cut from a dry sausage that came from the Alps, tomato, cucumber, baguette, and white-encrusted brie cheese. We ate, while the breeze goose-pimpled our skin, and the sun warmed us.

The contrast felt refreshing and kept me from dallying. I felt almost chilly enough to don a wind jacket over my shorts and t-shirt. Replenished by our snack; we easily cruised the mile or so to a lock on the outskirts of Agde. Here, we slid the kayak from the canal onto its wheels and strolled with it to the campground Patrick recommended. Life was easy.

At this lock, we would rinse off the salt of the Mediterranean Sea. From here we would paddle on freshwater channels until we approached the Atlantic. We would leave behind us the juicy oysters of the Étang de Thau. "Now," I expounded, *"The world is mine oyster, which I with my sword will open!"*[6] Then, turning to Kristin I asked, "Did you bring my sword?"

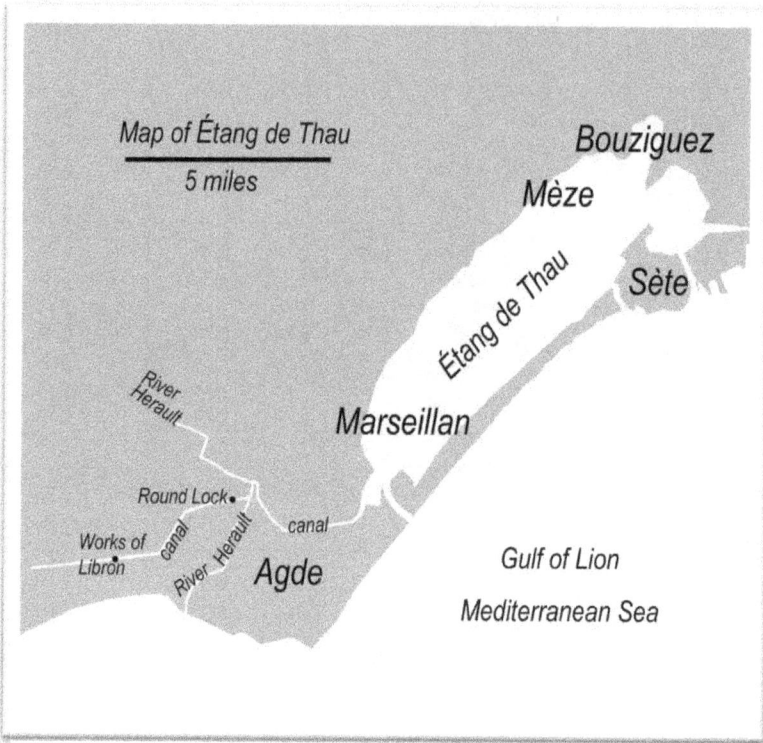

MAP 3. Étang de Thau.

4. Locks

A poor life this if, full of care
We have no time to stand and stare.[7]

Locks are wonderful contraptions for easy boating, offering a lift from one level of water to another, facilitating uphill travel. True, a current does run downhill through the locks toward the sea, but it is minimal, not a burden to paddle against like a river. But there is a procedure to follow at each lock.

Every lock has a chamber, large enough to hold at least one boat, with gates at both ends. Always, the gates and sluices must prevent all the water draining from the upper section of canal.

For a boat traveling upstream, the gates and sluices first shut at the upstream end of the lock. Water escapes from the lock through the sluices in the downstream gate. The water level must drop to that of the lower canal before the gates can open to admit the boat. Inside the lock, the crew moors the boat, holding its lines ready to adjust.

The downstream lock gates, and sluices, close before water fills the lock through the upstream sluices. The mooring lines, tensioned as the rising water lifts the boat, hold the boat against the current.

Once the water level in the lock reaches the level of the upstream canal, water stops flowing. The upstream gates open, the crew releases the mooring lines, and the boat is free to leave.

When another boat waits below the lock, then the upstream gates and sluices close again for the process to repeat.

It is an ingenious, and in theory simple, procedure to pass through a lock, but with plenty of details to frustrate a novice boater. Firstly, a lockkeeper may or may not be available to help. If there is one, the lockkeeper here will speak French, while many of the boaters we were to meet, of many nationalities, understood little or no French.

A pénichette enters a lock to descend.

A lockkeeper will help assure the novice that it is not okay to hit the open gate when steering to enter. Nor is it acceptable to run against the far gate to stop. He will do this by jumping up and down, gesticulating wildly and cursing loudly in French, undoubtably to calm whoever is trying to control the boat.

Locks

As soon as the crew has finished lashing the mooring lines securely to the bollards at the lock side, the lock keeper will stride across to untie them. Simply running each line around a bollard, he will pass control back to the blank-faced crew. Only then will he set the lock gates in motion, to slowly close.

Each lock might seem to have its own unique method of filling, yet there are only a few options. Some fill through ducts deep underwater, the incoming water welling up and mushrooming at the surface, sending out strong but quiet currents. Here, on the Canal du Midi, sluices in the gates allow plumes of water to gush into the lock, turning the surface into a frothing torrent resembling a whitewater river.

When novice boaters stand transfixed by the turbulence, the boat lifts on the rising water and the mooring lines slacken. The ever-watchful lockkeeper now strides up again to show the crew how to keep the lines taut, otherwise the current will carry the boat downstream against the gates. When the lock is full, the water stills. The lockkeeper opens the upstream gate, and watches the boat leave, wishing the next lockkeeper better luck.

Attentive crew tensions the line as the water rises.

Descending a lock is another matter. Should you tie off your lines to a bollard now, your boat will hang suspended by the mooring lines when the water empties.

Those who have watched the procedure many times can see why lockkeepers on the Canal du Midi need to take generously long lunch breaks. Nothing will persuade a lockkeeper to cut short lunch for an impatient boater.

A lunch time may inexplicably run into two hours. Experienced canal travelers, familiar with the routine, tie up, uncork a bottle or two of wine and settle down to a leisurely lunch. They show an abandon that suggests they are in no hurry to leave, ever. Their trick is to always carry enough wine, to always be vague about the day's destination, and to never ever pressurize the lockkeeper.

When cruising, it is difficult to guess how many boats will be waiting to use any given lock, or whether a particular lock will be under repair for an hour or two. Or how long the lockkeeper will need to drink wine at lunch to recover from the trauma of fielding novices. It is best to find a way to enjoy waiting.

Last night we stopped at an olive-shaped lock at days end, wheeling our kayak from there to the campground. Returning in the morning, we saw a boat negotiating the lock, climbing. On my earlier canal trip, Tim and I often leapfrogged the same barges day after day, starting our days earlier and finishing later than the faster barges. Today, we launched above the lock, and soon after, the boat from the lock passed us. I expected to see it again.

The canal runs across low land, the coastal plain, skirting to the north of Agde. At the next lock, seeing the gates open at both ends, we sped through, along the deep, stone-walled, corridor.

Joining the river Hérault, we paddled downstream for half a mile to where the canal branched away again to the west. A weir, just downriver from the junction, ensures sufficient depth of water for boat traffic. Everything was easy.

Locks

I had assumed we would rarely need to wait at Canal du Midi locks. There was plenty of room for more than one vessel inside an oval lock. Surely there would always be space for something extra, as small as a kayak.

An olive-shaped lock suggests an artistic flourish, a softening of the utilitarian rectangle more commonly seen, but that is not the motivation. Riquet redesigned his side walls to curve after one of his straight-sided locks collapsed inward. The oval shape is better able to resist the press of the adjacent land when the lock is empty.

We paddled on, confident in our prior knowledge of locks. Had not Tim and I negotiated 220 locks between the English Channel and the Mediterranean, in 1979? Surely, I could slip quietly through with Kristin without agitating the lockkeeper. The next lock proved me wrong.

"Non!" the lockkeeper announced most emphatically. "Kayaks are not allowed in the locks. Non! Non!"

"But we have our canal license. And we have been through locks before."

"No, kayaks are forbidden in the locks. No! Not in this one, not in any lock on the Canal du Midi. You will have to carry your kayak around." He turned his back and strode away.

I felt gutted. How many locks would we meet in the coming weeks? Something like 139? I had not bothered to count them accurately since the number was irrelevant: locks are integral to a canal journey. Could we carry our kayak around so many? At this lock we had no alternative. We got to work.

The easiest place to unload was against a tall concrete wall, at shoulder height when I stood in the kayak. I unloaded each hatch in turn, passing everything up to Kristin to stow into IKEA bags. Then I paddled the kayak to the gentlest bank, a little downstream from the lock. Determined, we slid the tandem up into the undergrowth, carried it to the path, up a flight of steps, over a fence and across a road.

We stood for a breather, sweating in the hot sun. The canal continued below the lock gates on the other side. A steep and high slope dropped to the water between trees. We could launch here. We lifted over another fence to lower the kayak at the end of a line to the water. Spotting an easier loading place, I paddled to the base of a long flight of steps on the opposite shore.

Having carried all our gear across the lock, and down to the kayak, we now began to stow everything. I was hot, and I was not happy. Going through the lock would have been so easy.

We were almost ready to leave, our kayak fully loaded, when I turned with a start. A man stood beside me on the steps. I had not heard him approach. He wore a skin-tight, black, neoprene wetsuit from head to toe, neck to wrist. He paused for a moment to take in the sight of our tandem kayak, then greeted us.

He sat down by the water. He took from under his arm a partly rounded plywood plate. This he began to strap onto his feet, like some enormous flipper. Then he readied his facemask and snorkel.

"Where are you going?" He asked.

"Toulouse, Bordeaux, the Atlantic Ocean." We replied nonchalantly.

He looked at us in astonishment, no doubt impressed that we would embark on such a journey by kayak. Then, as he lowered himself into the water, he said, "But this canal goes to Agde, to the Mediterranean." He pointed up the steps. "Toulouse is that way."

Then, fitting his snorkel into his mouth, mask checked and secure, he turned face-down and glided away through the water. With his plywood fin slowly beating like a manatee's tail, he aimed toward his sea.

I looked at Kristin. She looked at me. We had scarcely begun our journey and I had already lost our way. On a canal!

Locks

The wrong canal.

The lock we were portaging was the *Round Lock*. It features three entrances rather than the usual two. We were on a section of canal that led to the river Hérault, at Agde. From there, the river flows to the old port of Agde and finally to the sea. We had already paddled half a mile of the Hérault today, linking parts of the Canal du Midi. The route we were mistakenly taking would bypass the weir on the river. We began unloading the kayak, again.

Agde is another of the oldest towns in France, founded by Greek settlers from Massilia, (now Marseille) around 525 BC. Only Marseille, Marseillan and Béziers are known to be longer-established towns. Besides being known for its long history, Agde is notable for its naturist village, which hosts up to 50,000 naturists at a time. Referred to as a village, this town serves all the needs, if not all the desires of its visitors. At least, more than the bare necessities.

At midday, our kayak finally on the correct part of the canal and reloaded; Kristin asserted that she would paddle no farther before lunch. Across the road bridge by the round lock we found the bakery closed, but a stall sold us the few items we needed.

Perched at peace on the concrete wall above the calm waters of the canal, we uncorked a bottle of wine. With a penknife, we sliced avocados, tomatoes, fruit, honey bread, cheese, and salami. Our frustration over the portage turned into amusement, we snacked, waiting to see the first afternoon barge exit the lock.

Relaxed, I admitted to Kristin, "Tim and I missed a turning on our trip too. We ended up having to paddle back about two kilometers to where we should have turned."

"How on earth did you manage that?"

"We were wash-hanging: riding the boat wake. The large barges on those wide canals create a substantial stern wave. We just slipped in behind a barge and caught the wave. After that we only needed to steer. It was fun to ride the wave, although the exhaust fumes choked us.

"The kayak tended to surge forward on the wave, to ram the stern of the barge, so one of us reversed gently all the time. While I steered, Tim slouched back in his seat, got out the thermos flask and poured himself a cup of tea. He took his time drinking it, before passing the flask back to me. He took control of the kayak, while I sipped my tea and idly watched the shore slide by. The whole episode was pleasantly bizarre.

"The downside was, we enjoyed ourselves so much we missed our turning. Tim suddenly noticed the number on a kilometer mark beside the canal and realized how far we would have to paddle back."

5. Works of Libron

The triangle spins.
I see a circle
But I know it isn't so.[8]

The round lock is not round. Built circular in 1676, to allow barges to turn to either exit, a later extension to accommodate larger vessels left it lopsided. The builders chose volcanic stone for this construction, which seems odd, since the surrounding countryside is composed of sedimentary rocks. Yet some imposing buildings in nearby Agde, such as the cathedral, used basalt too. The stone comes from the hill at Agde, Mont Saint-Loup, the last in a chain of volcanoes stretching south from the once volcanically active Massif Central.

If I thought the shape of the round lock was special, I found the next lock, some four miles farther along the coastal plain, even more extraordinary. Here, the early canal operators faced a problem where the canal crosses the diminutive Libron river. The canal elevation is scarcely higher than that of the river. When the Libron flooded, it filled the canal with debris. The canal required dredging after each flood before traffic could pass: an inconvenience, since flash floods occurred up to twenty times each year. Could they find a better remedy?

Kayak across France

The first solution was a flat-topped barge which, when sunk, filled the canal up to the brim. End walls on the barge channeled the water across. The barge, refloated and moved away as soon as the floodwater dropped, left the waterway clear of debris, but it forced traffic to wait for the duration of each flood.

The engineer, Urbain Maguès, finally came up with an ingenious solution to allow traffic during floods. He built the elaborate Works of Libron in 1855. He divided the river through two culverts under the canal. He partitioned the canal above into a row of three chambers. Each outer chamber has sluices on all four sides. In times of flood, all the canal sluices close and the river overflow sluices open. The river runs across the two outer chambers of the canal, leaving the inner one enclosed and calm.

When a boat needs to pass the Works, the river overflow sluices of the nearest river channel close, diverting the river through the far channel. The nearest two sets of canal sluices open to allow the boat to enter the central chamber. When those canal sluices close again behind the boat, the river sluices behind reopen to allow the river to flow through both channels again.

Next, the river overflow sluices of the chamber ahead of the boat close, diverting all the river across the chamber behind the boat. When the final two sets of canal sluices open, the boat is free to continue along the canal. Finally, those canal sluices shut, the overflow sluices open, and the river uses both channels again.

Arriving when the river was low, we found all the canal sluices open. We paddled beneath elegant arches of yellowish sandstone, or limestone, which cast bold shadow patterns across the water. The sun, beaming down between, set the translucent green water aglow. The splash of our paddles echoed from the side chambers, where waves slapped and licked against stone. In the shade, the draughty air chilled my skin.

I looked around. The roofless space, enclosed by stone buttresses and arches, was carpeted in rippling green. It was reminiscent of a derelict church, reminding me of Piranesi's drawings of ruins, although the Works of Libron, far from ruined, is a feat of engineering in full working order.

Works of Libron.

At the exit, we tethered our kayak to the stone wall and climbed up to see the top of the structure. Here was the mechanical apparatus, with giant cogs, levers, chains, and tracks, used to control the sluices. A masterpiece precursor of steampunk.

Below, murky water flowed slowly from the culverts beneath the canal, joining to become a ditch rather than a river. I thought back to my first canal trip, where winter rains had caused extensive flooding. Here, it is summer storms, particularly in August, which cause flash floods.

Who controls this contraption? Who makes sure the canal sluices stay open whenever the river is low? Someone closes the canal and opens the river sluices when the river floods. A lockkeeper's cottage stood on the uphill side, but was it occupied?

I expect so, since the Works must need constant maintenance to be ready for the occasional flood. Could I operate these gates in the correct sequence if I had to? It would take some time to figure out how.

Operating Mechanism, Works of Libron.

A single, sometimes double, line of plane trees now ran along each side of the canal. A continuous leafy canopy spread beside and above the canal, supported by pale mottled tree trunks. Each tree grew close enough to its neighbor for the roots to knit together, firmly securing the canal bank. The dappled green tunnel lay mirrored in the canal. This narrowed into the distance to where a punch-hole of light glowed from a single bridge arch.

Farmland, with vineyards, stretched away beyond the shelter of the canal. Cyclists cranked along a track, half-hidden by the trees and an embankment. Sometimes they spotted us, waved, and called out a greeting in passing.

The canal ran across low and level ground, leaving me plenty of time to consider how to tackle the locks ahead. We would negotiate the locks on foot if we must. But I was delighted when an English couple, from West London, suggested an alternative. Marilyn, and Trevor Westoll, were at the start of their adventure and had boarded their rental boat shortly before we met them at their first lock. Trevor wondered, since the lockkeepers here allow boats to tow a tender into the locks, then why not a kayak? "It's probably forbidden to ride in it," he cautioned. "But, worth a try?"

Kristin got out and ran to ask the *éclusier*, lockkeeper, for permission. She hurried back, excited to announce that yes, he would allow it. Kristin helped Marilyn to ready the boat's mooring lines, while I tied our own line between the kayak's bow and one of its side handles. I crouched on the boat's low stern platform to tow and steer the kayak, while the boat slowly entered the lock and moored.

Once the lock was full, and the gates open, Trevor motored slowly out and dropped us ashore. He then cruised on ahead. The process had been quick and easy, unlike our pantomime at the round lock.

Gradually we approached busier, and noisier, territory where boats had parked for the long term. Then, at Villeneuve-lès-Béziers, we caught up with Trevor and Marilyn, waiting their turn to enter a lock. Once again, they kindly towed our kayak through. Dusk was now approaching, when locks would close for the night, so Trevor suggested we camped nearby when they found somewhere to overnight.

We brought our kayak onshore by the boat and pitched our tent beneath plane trees. Then, scaling Trevor and Marilyn's narrow gangplank, we joined them for beverages and snacks in their cabin. They regaled us with stories from their narrow boat journeys on English canals, and their balloon trip and gliding experiences. Adventurous, they had traveled widely and were animated storytellers. Time and wine slipped by with each new story until, the night now late, we gingerly crossed the gangplank to our tent.

Awake before light, I reflected how comfortably warm I felt these September mornings. I listened to the erratic rhythm of a nearby sign swinging in the night wind. Trains and road traffic punctuated a farmyard chorus of cockerels, ducks, and dogs. The noises blended into a comforting ambient sound.

For some reason, I recalled feeling the same self-indulgent relaxation long ago in London. I awoke there to the sound of someone in the nearby kitchen. Water gushed from a faucet into a thin metal kettle. When the faucet turned off; water dripped a hollow heartbeat into a deep stone sink. The kettle clunked down onto a gas hob: a match rasped against the box and fizzed into flame.

I heard the clack of a heavy stove key turn, followed by the powerful hiss of town gas. With a whoosh, the gas ignited. Content then, I lay curled and comfortable in an unfamiliar bed. There was no immediate reason to stir, so I lay there in anticipation of the kettle's steam whistle.

Here too I felt comfortable, and lazy, but soon turned on my side and lit my headlamp to consult our map. I was curious to scout our path ahead, eager to anticipate what the coming day might hold.

Outside in the early freshness, I stood with Kristin to watch the yellowish glow from the sun climb down the plane trees beside the canal. Stepping toward the kayak, our feet crunched the hand-sized, gently arched, scabby flakes of exfoliated plane tree bark. I thought of them as giant potato chips. Miniature pomanders lay among the slender grasses, burdocks, and fallen twigs: the pale, spherical studded seed heads fallen from the plane trees.

The canal here ran through an avenue of plane trees. Their sturdy trunks revealed patches of smooth pale grey-green bark, wherever the mottled dark grey and brown patches of older bark had peeled and fallen away. Plane trees have an effective strategy to repel epiphytes. Any mosses, lichens, or ferns, which might smother the tree, fall away when the bark dries, cracks, and flakes. As each flake falls away, it exposes fresh new bark underneath. In this way, plane trees were able to survive the nineteenth century industrial smoke, and smog, in London, England, while other species choked beneath a layer of soot.

Boat under Bridge.

I balanced the stove on the kayak seat pad, with the espresso maker perched on top. The pad was the most secure place I could create. Soon a jet of rich brown liquid filled the waiting cup. I was still daydreaming at breakfast with Kristin when Trevor appeared cheerfully from the cabin of his boat. He bid us farewell, hauled in his gangplank and mooring lines, and left us alone.

Canal travel differs from sea kayaking in that there is an exact predetermined route. Boats move along the canal in waves, catching up with each other and slowing, clumping together. They wait their turn at each lock, which spreads them apart again. The overall motion of multiple boats reminds me of that of an earthworm.

Some people motor along slowly, often pausing to cycle along the shore, stroll, or picnic. Others bustle urgently onward but stop early in the evening. Overall, no matter the strategy, all boats average about the same speed. Consequently, reaching a junction at the first lock of our day, I was not surprised to recognize the lively crew on a Pénichette waiting there.

We had watched this boat, *Campignol,* pass us near Étang du Thau, while we ate lunch on first joining the canal. They invited us aboard, where we learned their names: Nanou, Jacky, Chantal, and Pascal. Then they prepared to tow our kayak through the lock, to save us a portage.

Pénichette, French Group.

The lock chamber was a deep, dark, straight-sided slot. Inside the lock, the damp air smelled like marsh mud, boat exhaust, and yesterday's stale breakfast. With my line, I was able to maneuver the kayak alongside the boat to allow a second boat to enter behind. The gates closed to shut us into the gloomy box. With a roar, water gushed in, and spray flew. The surface boiled and churned; my ears filled with the commotion. Echoey laughter rang out loud in the stone-walled enclosure. Excited voices from both boats called out a commentary.

We rose gradually until, near the top, the light brightened to a new dawn. Soon, the lockkeepers house alongside became visible over the lip. A few passersby stood watching us appear.

The boat eased from the lock to a new view: a broader stretch of water a quarter mile long. Boats and barges had moored along the shores, while low buildings stood behind a line of trees. Another narrow, straight-sided, lock stood at the far end of the pool, open, ready for us to enter.

These two rectangular locks, the one ahead and the one behind, improve on Riquet's route. His way had turned left where we entered the first lock. Traffic, taking that route, used to enter the river Orb upstream of a barrage built to maintain sufficient water level. Boats pushed a half mile upstream to reenter the canal on the far side, before climbing steeply through locks. The first few of those locks, disused, now block that way.

Our next lock on the new route so close, we stayed on the boat all the way through. Then our friends pulled aside briefly to let us disembark. We waved, and called, "Bon Voyage et Merci!" and with a little sadness watched them accelerate away.

A few yards ahead stood the longest aqueduct on the Canal du Midi. Béziers, almost hidden from here, clad the hill to the north and east.

Water filling a lock.

6. Béziers

Into these stones
their sorrow spilled,
As twenty thousand
hearts were stilled.[9]

Béziers must have presented a formidable challenge to Pierre-Paul Riquet. Here, at the inland edge of the coastal plain, the valley of the river Orb cuts through an escarpment. Béziers, with its creamy stonework and orange roof-tiles, covers the hill to one side, crowning it with the square tower of the solidly constructed cathedral of Saint Nazaire. Across the river stands another hill. Somehow, Riquet's canal had to cross the river and climb the hill.

The river Orb was sometimes too low for navigation where the canal joined, so Riquet constructed a barrage to hold a minimum level. From a short distance upriver, he led the canal up the steep hill, opposite Béziers, through a series of nine locks: the Fonserannes Locks.

The first of those locks allowed boats to enter from river level. From there, after a short section of canal, a continuous flight of eight, connected, locks climbed eighty-six feet in fewer than 350 yards. The total nine locks gave the Fonserannes Locks another name, *the rise of nine.*

Riquet's barrage could hold back a head of water deep enough for boats, and his locks could handle a climb, but sometimes the river's strong currents stopped traffic for weeks on end. It took all but two hundred years before an alternative route, the aqueduct, opened to traffic in 1858.

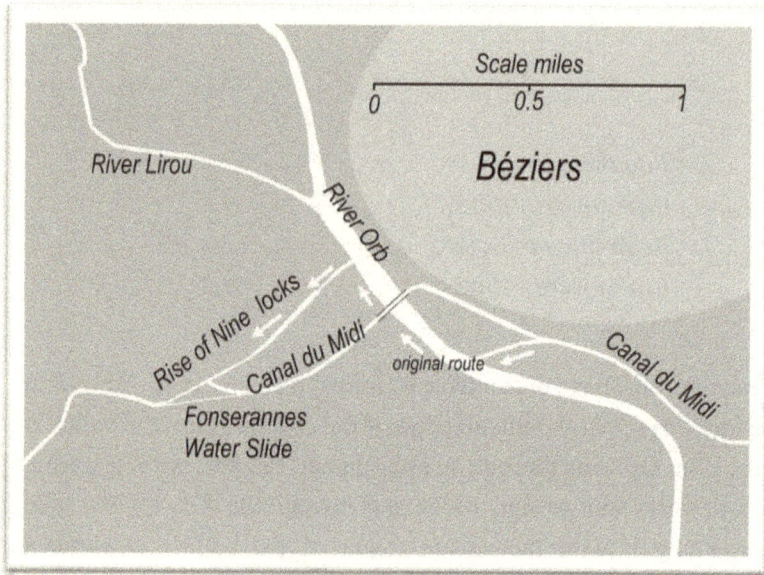

MAP 4. Canal route past Béziers.

Béziers is an ancient city dating from 575 BC, making it even older than Agde. It is second in age to Marseille, the oldest city in France. People have occupied the site at Béziers since Neolithic times. It saw the coming of Celts, and then Romans, before becoming part of Muslim Iberia for a time. But it is associated most memorably with Catharism,

Catharism, a Christian dualist movement, first took hold around here in the city of Albi, so Cathar followers were often known as Albigensian. Cathars held different, and often opposing, views to those held by the Roman Catholic church. They scorned the wealth and pageantry of the Roman Catholic order. The movement became widespread in the wealthy Languedoc by the twelfth century. As Catharism grew more popular, it seemed possible that it would become more widespread than Catholicism, threatening the coffers and powerful hierarchy of the Roman Catholic church.

Pope Innocent III, then head of the Catholic church, sent missionaries to quash Catharism, but they failed. In 1209 he called for a formal Albigensian crusade, and the Northern French barons came at his service to wipe out the Cathar religion by force.

Since Catholics and Cathars lived in peace together in Languedoc, communities simply refused to reveal Cathars to the crusaders. It became expedient for the invaders to kill everyone rather than discover who held which Christian belief. This crusade caused the deaths of an estimated half million Languedoc people. Many killed were Cathars, but the crusaders slaughtered countless Catholic men, women, and children too.

History tells how the Cistercian abbot, Arnaud Amaury, gave the command, "Kill them all, God will know his own." His order led to the ultimate slaughter of every inhabitant of the city of Béziers, and anyone else who had fled there for shelter. That was an estimated twenty thousand people. I found it difficult to look across at the city on the hill, now dominated by the Catholic cathedral, without feeling sadness at such atrocity.

Catholic forces continued to persecute Cathars until, after two hundred years, there was almost no sign of the religion. The crusade, first begun against the Cathar religion, became an excuse to take territory for France. Now impoverished Languedoc, formerly the wealthiest region of Europe, was destined to become the poorest region of France.

The aqueduct at Béziers now carries the canal across the river Orb. Supported thirty-nine feet above the river (12 meters), by seven stone arches, the structure spreads ninety-two feet wide including towpaths on either side, (28 meters). Beneath each towpath runs an arcaded walkway for pedestrians. These, no longer open to the public, have become a gathering place for flocks of pigeons.

Aqueduct at Béziers.

It felt strange to kayak across a bridge, but the feeling was in my head only. I knew we were high above the river, but I could not see past the wall beside the towpath from our low viewpoint. Having crossed the river, we stood on the towpath behind the chest-high stone wall to see the river Orb flowing peacefully below.

Then we climbed down the steps to the riverbank to view the aqueduct arches mirrored into circles in the calm water. Young willows, and alders, thrived at the base of the stonework where each arch stood in the river. Here, the riverbank was peaceful, sheltered from noise and breeze, tempting me to linger longer, but we were keen to tackle the flight of locks that awaited.

Béziers

After a half mile of tree-lined canal, on the outside of a bend, we found a ramp that sloped steeply uphill between vertical concrete walls. The ramp was the width of a lock. A short distance up the slope stood a massive, blue-painted, metal bridge structure. At its downhill end, a huge black plate; a raised guillotine-style gate or giant sluice, left the entrance open.

No boat could climb the slope to enter such a lock. Instead, the blue locomotive must descend on its eighteen big wheels to the buffers at the base. The gate lifted; a boat could float underneath into the end of the channel at the base of the slope.

With the gate closed behind, the powerful engine takes about six minutes to carry a boat to the top of the slope, pushing it on its capsule of water. There, a set of standard lock gates lets the boat reenter the canal.

This ingenious shortcut bypassed a laborious climb through multiple locks. The Fonserannes water slope, or *Pente d'eau,* began its timesaving service to commercial traffic in 1983, for an added fee.

All did not always run smoothly. I heard of one accident when the contraption ran downhill out of control, causing a wave to rush along the canal and across the aqueduct. The wave caused havoc with the boats on the canal beyond. The ramp stopped service in 2001 and has been idle ever since.

Opposite the *Pente d'eau*, about seven boats lingered loosely at the bank, fenders dangling ready. Bicycles adorned the decks. People, some dressed in shorts and bikini tops, basked in the sun, others relaxed in the shade beneath blue parasols. Some called from boat to boat, the sound of their laughter rippling across the water. Among those waiting were our French friends, also Trevor and Marilyn.

Trevor told us that one of the lock gates had broken, and how a repair team, he pointed out their white van, was already there working on it. Until they finished work, nobody could pass in either direction. He helped us slide our kayak from the water. He was intrigued by how easily our trolly wheels, which stowed between my feet and the bulkhead, clipped onto the cradle I kept handy in the cockpit under my knees. Then he saw how we lifted one end of the kayak to slip the trolley underneath.

Here, Kristin and I had both an advantage and a disadvantage over the others. We were free to continue, but having crossed the neglected section of canal, which once led traffic up from the river, we faced a steep climb. Our way ahead, devoid of sheltering trees, was sunbaked.

The locks, from number one at the top, count past the unused lock number eight where we soon stood, to number nine, close to the river. Boats from the aqueduct enter the rise at lock number seven, which is permanently open at the side, reaching the lowest used lock in the flight, number six, to begin the climb.

We began pushing our kayak, toiling up the canal-side road, past a café, past lock after lock, step by sun-seared step until we reached the top. Red-faced and perspiring from the exertion, we took a breather beside a dory on the canal quay. Repurposed, the dory overflowed with shrubs and flowering plants. The scent from the bright flowers hung sweet and heavy in the air, amid the murmur of bees.

"Let's go back to the café," Kristin suggested wearily. "We need to rehydrate." So, we plodded downhill to find a table for two. Shaded by an umbrella beside the building, we ordered water, red wine, and paninis. Gradually relaxing as we cooled down, we lingered over our wine until the clamor of voices warned us that boats had begun to climb the locks, the repair complete.

A crowd of spectators gathered to watch each small boat maneuver through the narrow entrance into position in the lozenge shaped lock, leaving room for one behind, and two on the other side. As soon as the gates closed behind, the froth of whitewater cascaded from above, filling the lock.

Once the uphill gates opened, the boats, one by one, squeezed through into the next lock. Soon boats filled all the locks. Every boat climbed uphill, and none descended, although boats can, and do, pass simultaneously through the locks in both directions.

Cooled and refreshed, we followed the trail of boats, climbing slowly from lock to lock, watching, and listening to the excited banter. Our kayak awaited at the top beside the boatful of flowers, while ahead, Riquet's canal resumed its original route. We skimmed across the reflections, looking down at the foliage shading us overhead. All was quiet, all was calm.

Flight of locks at Béziers.

Malpas Tunnel.

7. Ensérune and the Tunnels

That day is fixed most firmly in my memory,
seeing how our return journey was set to be the
first one underground...[10]

Three and a half miles past the Béziers rise of locks, we reached the village Colombiers. Here a canal marina offered a sheltered pool for boats to rest with harbor facilities, where people can start a canal trip in a rented boat. The village being beside the canal, we assumed we could buy supplies, but not, we discovered, at that time of day. The boulangerie had closed and so had the supermarket. During lunchtime we were unable to buy anything.

One mile beyond Colombiers marina the canal enters a deep, steep-sided, cutting in the side of a hill and then disappears into Malpas tunnel. Dressed stone clads the cliff around and above the entrance and lines the northeastern part of the tunnel to prevent rockfalls. The southwestern section is unlined, exposing sandstone that has weathered into a wonderfully crinkled texture. A towpath runs along one side but extends only as far as the stonework of the lined section. I imagine it once ran all the way through until that stone facing took up the width of the towpath.

Malpas canal tunnel is reputedly the oldest canal tunnel in Europe, if not the world, although not the first tunnel through this hill, nor the latest. Monks tunneled from the north in the mid-thirteenth century to drain water from Étang de Montady. That lake, or by then marsh, was a breeding ground for disease. The 1,364-meter-long tunnel, at a lower level than Riquet's, was two meters high and a half meter wide.

Riquet's tunneling team broke through some vertical ventilation shafts, and found they led down to the earlier tunnel. Instead of sealing the holes, the canal builders plugged the shafts, leaving a convenient way to drain the canal for maintenance. Then, water would fall some ten meters into the older channel to drain away.

Riquet's tunnel measures 165 meters long, having an arched roof that reaches eight meters above the water. The most recent tunnel, dug through the hill in the mid-1800s for the railway, measures 504 meters.

If the cool passage through the tunnel captured our immediate imagination, there was more to see here. Securing our kayak, we climbed a dusty track to the road, Sturdy grasshoppers whirred loudly, rattling, and crackling as they took to the air on crisp banded wings when we approached. The hot, dusty air dried my throat and the glare from the pale earth between the spiky vegetation made me squint despite my sunglasses.

The road climbed to the ancient Gallic-Roman hilltop town, Oppidum d'Ensérune. This town occupied the hilltop for some seven hundred years, from the sixth century BC, until the inhabitants abandoned it in the first century AD, moving to lower ground.

Ensérune lay between Béziers and Narbonne on the route of the Via Domitia. Coming from Italy, this road went on to thread a pass in the Pyrenees on its way to the Iberian Peninsula. Ensérune became a military staging place on the way, with the construction of a fort.

Oppidum d'Ensérune is now a preserved archaeological site. A museum here houses some of the ancient finds and explains the layout of the remains and the history. But it is easy to see how attractive the hilltop would have been to settlers. It offers sweeping views across the coastal plain to the Mediterranean and the Pyrenees on one side. At the base of the hill on the other side was once the Étang de Montady.

The coastal plain around the Gulf of Lyon has a string of such étangs, brackish lakes or saltwater lagoons, from the Camargue to the Pyrenees. These lakes were a source of fish, game birds, and salt. Many still survive. Étang de Montady, drained and converted into farmland in Medieval times, lives on in name only.

Étang de Montady seen from oppidum.

From above, Étang de Montady bears the striking appearance of a buckled spoked wheel, the irregular rim in the original shape of the marsh. The spokes, straight drainage ditches, converge on a central circular ditch and track: the wheel hub. They divide the land into sixty or so narrow field segments, minutes on a clock face or degrees on a compass. Broader ditches cut the central disk unevenly, defining four fields in a pattern that resembles a ban-the bomb sign. From the very center runs a broader channel which almost reaches the entrance to the railway tunnel.

I understand that water drains down sixteen vertical shafts to a culvert, in a design like a Persian qanat. The culvert. leads to the tunnel beneath the hill. The drainage system is still functional, the tunnel now serendipitously connected via its ventilation shafts to Riquet's canal tunnel. The farmland, reclaimed by draining Étang de Montady, yields crops including grapes.

The remains of the hilltop town and Roman fort, spread east-west along a ridge. The foundations and low walls reveal the layout of the settlement, and the floorplans of the buildings, in a giant circuit board of low, cream-colored, stone.

The voices of the people who positioned these stones to build their homes have been silent for more than two millennia. Would they have spoken Latin? Julius Caesar once complimented the people of Aquitaine, in southwest France, on speaking better Latin than those in Rome. I imagine people would have spoken mostly Latin here too. Eventually it would evolve into Occitan, the language of d'Òc, Languedoc.

Exploring the defensive walls we passed a level area of ground pocked by holes, each surrounded by a smooth ceramic rim protruding above the ground. These looked so clean and regular I assumed they were recent; I guessed ventilation for something underneath. But they were openings to ancient underground storage silos for grain, wine, or oil. The storage was easily accessible, while a stone effectively closed the hole. Wet clay spread around the stone dried into a protective seal. There are some three hundred silos here.

Throughout Ensérune, archaeological excavations have yielded all manner of artifacts including amphorae to hold wine or olive oil. Some of these, with other items such as funerary urns, military buckles, and swords, are on display in the small museum.

Ensérune and the tunnels

The air was dry, and we carried no water, so the idea of a chilled beverage tempted us. Below the hill we saw canopy-shaded tables, beside a café where we found refreshments.

The tunnels through the hillside reminded me of the 1979 canal trip Tim and I made. Then, canal officials would not allow us to paddle through the first tunnel we reached. Russian prisoners had built that tunnel during Napoléonic times. It was three and a half miles long. Since horses towed the canal barges then, ventilation was adequate, but it is insufficient for modern, motorized, barges.

Nowadays, to eliminate the hazard of diesel fumes, an electric *cheval*: winch boat, powered like a trolly-bus via overhead cables, tows a string of fifteen to twenty barges through, every evening. Each morning it tows a train of barges in the opposite direction.

The barges starting their tunnel journey in the evening, spend the night parked at the far end before traveling on. But a second tunnel follows a short distance after their resting place. The canal official would not allow us to paddle through that one either.

Since we faced a long, and awkward, portage, he kindly asked a barge owner to carry our kayak through and then drove us to the far end, where we camped. There, we reclaimed our kayak next morning when the barge emerged from the second tunnel.

We negotiated more tunnels in the days ahead, but these we were able to paddle through. The one near Rheims was 1.4 miles long. One between the Marne valley and the Saône extended three miles. They were so long; the far end was not discernable in the distance. Under the glow of the occasional lamp above the canal, we discovered what made the scuffling sounds all along the towpath, high alongside. Lots of big rats.

On the Canal du Midi, the Malpas tunnel, in contrast to the earlier ones I had seen, seemed ancient, cave-like, and quaint.

From the Malpas tunnel, the Canal du Midi contours the edge of the coastal plain. Beyond one shoulder, the land rose in an embankment and hill. On the other side spread farmland. We followed the canal's twists into the pretty village of Poilhes.

A red, cigar-shaped, shop sign hung above a tobacconist: *tabac*. I recognized the sign from early French lessons at school, but Kristin saw the café table nearby in the narrow street. Scrambling ashore, leaving the kayak in my care, she soon returned smiling, brandishing a baguette, and carrying a pastry.

While we snacked on the pastry, Pascal, and the group from his boat, all dressed up for an evening ashore, came strolling along the road toward us, calling out and laughing. It was fun to greet such a happy crowd.

It must be a marvelous experience to step off a boat for an evening ashore, at a village, dressed and prepared for a night out, compared to how we set up our tent in a quiet rural place, to bed down at nightfall.

Our snack was so tasty, Kristin ran back to buy another pastry: our equivalent of a night on the town. Then, passing Pascal's empty boat, we sought a quiet place, between a wooded slope and the towpath,

Kristin chose an easy egress onto grass and crispy plane bark. Finding nowhere flat, we pitched the tent across the slope in the place most free of briars and tiny sharp rose plants.

Climbing the slope through the undergrowth we reached a narrow lane, alongside a smallholding growing grape vines and tomatoes. The sun was low. We leaned back against a tree, a bottle of wine, a baguette, cheese, and sausage spread on a mat beside us, with fresh cucumber and tomato. The fire of the sunset glowed up from the water between the dark reflected stripes of the regimented row of silhouetted trees opposite.

8. Capestang

To market to market
To buy what we will
Home again home again
Hungrier still.[11]

It is only five winding kilometers from Poilhes to Capestang, a town named after another étang. Suddenly, in contrast to the pale dappling of the plane trees, here the somber tall dark slender pencils of cypress trees lined the canal. Behind stood the massive block tower of the heavily buttressed thirteenth century, unfinished, collegiate church, standing like a castle.

Capestang sits on the slope above the extensive wetlands that once formed the étang de Capestang, yet most of the town lies below the level of the canal. In 1766 during heavy storms, the canal traffic halted and that meant the locks stopped releasing water. The buildup of water in the canal burst the banks above Capestang causing a disastrous flood through the town.

After that, stronger banks, and an allowance for runoff, have prevented the canal overfilling and flooding again. There have been no floods since.

Leaving our kayak tied alongside the quay, we took a shower at the canal office building. Our camera batteries charging at the tourist information desk, we walked to the Capestang open market to shop. Here were stalls neatly displaying colorful fruit and vegetables. Others showed brightly colored cloth bags and clothes. Each stall sheltered from the sun beneath the trees and colorful umbrellas.

Kristin buying produce at Capestang.

Having found a boulangerie for the requisite baguettes, we threaded the narrow streets, houses opening directly to the street, to find the collegiate church on the site of the eleventh century église de Saint Étienne. There is little visible of the earlier church, for most of its stone was repurposed in the towering building that replaced it.

The outer walls of that fifteenth century construction reach for the skies, supported by massive stone buttresses and flying buttresses. Gargoyles peer down from above. Inside, stained glass windows and chandeliers spread light on the altar. We climbed a cool, narrow, echoey stone stairway to a balcony, to look out into the cavernous nave. Far below were the rows of pews, tiny pews for the tiny people as they appeared to be from up here.

Kristin, having studied art history at university, wanted to visit the castle of the Archbishops of Narbonne in Capestang. "They have a painted ceiling which is supposed to be quite special!" she tempted. The chateau, an unimposing low building, stood nearby, a police station built onto the end. We entered to find a chilly hall. The pale stucco had crumbled away in places to expose rough stone walls. A simple open fireplace dominated the far end of the hall, while tall, walled-up, arches along one side restricted the natural light to that coming from smaller, arched, windows.

A later addition to the twelfth century hall is a wooden ceiling installed in the fifteenth century. The long ceiling beams, lavishly decorated, glowed golden-red. The finely scribed, painted patterns caught my eye. They reminded me of Māori tattoos, in charcoal blue-black, but also in dulled, bloodstain, red.

Studying the beams I saw depictions of amusing imaginary beings, anthropomorphized creatures, and a naked woman eaten by two wide-jawed beasts. There were portrayals of long-legged, long-beaked, heron-like birds: most likely egrets. Also, human couples in Medieval attire, and greyhounds. Up close I could see the artists had used many colors, despite my first impression. I imagine the colors were brighter when first painted in the late Middle Ages. Such a ceiling must have been a spectacular addition to a furnished hall hung with textiles.

Gazing up, I felt the centuries of religious faith concertina in and out. Here, as at Béziers, a community of both Cathars and Roman Catholics once lived in peace.

The Albigensian Crusade, and the inquisition that followed, had completely eradicated the Cathars by 1350. From that time, Languedoc began to be a part of France, under the French monarchy. Prudent people took pains to appear to be Roman Catholic.

This hall stood here before that conflict began. Afterwards, Capestang was firmly under the control of one of the long succession of Archbishops of Narbonne who owned this property. The painters of the luscious ceiling, illustrating egrets and hounds, would not have witnessed the elimination of Cathars a century before. But that bloodshed must have permeated the collective memory.

Returning to the canal, to my dismay, I found the doors to the tourist information center firmly locked. Closed for lunch, they would not reopen until two in the afternoon. Since we had to wait to retrieve our camera batteries, we found a bench and sat facing the canal to eat our own lunch.

"I remember in England when I was growing up," I reminisced, "how businesses used to close for lunch. Few places opened at all on a Sunday. Now I expect everything to stay open all day long, and all weekend. It never crosses my mind they might close for lunch here! How many times have we been caught out already?"

As we sipped the rest of last night's wine, picnicking on bread, cheese and fruit, people passing wished us a friendly "bon appétit!"

The canal continued its wonderfully wiggly way through the countryside, contouring the hillside without any locks. At the junction to the Canal du Robine, we paused for a moment. Its highest lock stood just a couple of hundred yards away.

"Let's have a look," I suggested, curious to see more of the Robine. We made the turn toward the lock, and soon climbed the bank to look down along Robine's next section.

All was quiet. Close below the lock a man stood on the overgrown shore grilling beside his moored boat. Pale wispy smoke spiraled into the trees. We sat on a wall to rest for a moment. Swallows sped by, swept, and glided above the water, a gleam of blue-black, a twist of white underside. Below them, ripples showed where insects or fish plucked the surface. The calm scene reminded me of a rural English river wandering through summer farmland.

The waterway leads to Narbonne, the ecclesiastical and strategic center of this corner of Languedoc. Beyond Narbonne, the canal du Robine continues until it reaches the Mediterranean.

At one time Narbonne was a bustling port. When the Romans built the town in 118 BC, it stood on one of two exit branches of the Aude River. To use the town as a Mediterranean port, they built a ship canal, from the mouth of the river at Narbonne, across the Bages-Sigean lagoon, to the sea.

Adopted for a time by Julius Caesar as his home port, Narbonne was also at an important Roman road junction. Here, the Via Aquitania, which led to the Atlantic, branched from the Via Domitia, which connected Rome to Spain.

Narbonne declined in significance as a port after the Aude changed its course and the waterway access to the Mediterranean silted up. That prompted the construction of La Robine, to supply water to Narbonne. Connected to the Canal du Midi much later, in 1776, the waters meet here.

As I stood in front of the lockkeeper's house, I saw a signpost with three arrows. I assumed it was for boat traffic. One way pointed right, to Carcassonne, another left, to Narbonne, but the third, to Béziers, aimed across the canal. Surely Béziers and Carcassonne should both be in the direction of the Canal du Midi? But then I realized, the sign was for cyclists, not for boats. Cyclists bound for Béziers, along the Mediterranean side of the Canal du Midi, must detour to cross the lock here.

We rejoined the Canal du Midi, continuing along its tree-lined way toward the next village, La Somail. It is a winding section of canal. Of the thirteen miles (22km) we would paddle from Capestang to La Somail, a crow would need to fly just eight. Our paddle strokes in time, blades slipping quietly in and out of the water, we chatted about nothing, called greetings to cyclists on the bank, and looked out across farmland. But we slowed when we reached La Somail.

Beside a large building enveloped in a coat of green creepers, a huge barge was inching toward us, blocking the gap beneath a bridge. It did not look as if it would fit. It appeared too wide. Clearly, we must wait. Meanwhile the sound of live music drifted through the air, the sound of an accordion, a cello, drums, voices singing. A distinctively French musical sound.

We slumped back in our seats, relaxed. To our left, a sign beside the canal outside a barn offered wine tasting.

"Maybe we should stop and taste some wine." Kristin tempted. "Or we could go through the bridge first if you like, to see if there's somewhere better?" She loves to offer options. I chose to wait for the barge.

9. Big Barges

The barge she sat in,
like a burnish'd throne,
Burned on the water:
the poop was beaten gold;
Purple the sails, and so perfumed that
The winds were lovesick with them...[12]

The barge emerged gradually, defying all my expectations as it slowly grew. It seemed a phenomenally long barge for this canal, and I wondered how it managed the locks. It must, of course, otherwise how could it have got here?

"Any bigger and it could never pass that bridge!" I shook my head. Drifting, I looked around. To our left, a faded blue sit-on-top kayak was idly floating, loosely tied at the bank below outdoor tables. A long-haired, slender, young woman in a figure-hugging black dress stood at ease, a glass of white wine in her hand, talking to someone I could not see. Evening here was the time to relax, to socialize outside in the warm, dry, air after work or study.

As even more of the barge appeared from under the bridge, I began to wonder exactly how long it could be. Later I learned that the *Alouette* was a cargo barge built in 1908, converted to a luxury hotel barge in 1986. Owned and managed by Orient Express Hotels, (Since 2014, Belmond), she carries a maximum of four passengers. The crew of four consists of captain, hostess, tour guide and chef.

In length, the *Alouette* was close to the maximum possible. Riquet's canal locks measured one hundred feet long and the *Alouette* is ninety-eight feet long, leaving only one foot of clearance at each end. The entrance to a Riquet lock was nineteen feet eight inches wide. The *Alouette's* beam, at seventeen feet, left a margin of just sixteen inches to either side when entering or leaving.

The Alouette at La Somail.

Once our way was clear and we sped under the bridge, the volume of music and chatter seemed to soar, invigorating me. The band was on the left bank, people pausing and gathering to listen. Artists at easels stood brush in hand, curious passersby peering over their shoulders to compare the painting to the scene. Some revelers clustered, holding glasses. Others gazed along the canal as the crowd slowly drifted, like sand through an hourglass, over the bridge, between the crowds on either bank. The mood was inviting!

Having slid our kayak ashore just beyond the festivities, we walked back to learn that the party was in celebration of the tenth anniversary of the café beside the bridge. The café was in the building smothered in climbing plants.

The animated band consisted of a woman, who played accordion and sang, a drummer and a cellist. They played confidently without watching their instruments, turning their heads to nod at acquaintances, interacting with the audience, aware of all that was going on. In contrast, the artists behind easels appeared to be self-absorbed. They made scarcely a gesture, except to the canvas: to freeze a moment of the scene. In view: the bridge and party crowd.

Live music beside canal.

We meandered happily, our mood energized by the music, past the outdoor tables of the café restaurant. Extra people joined those already crowding the tables, and many turned their chairs to face the band. Passing them and rounding the corner of the building, we stepped into shade and diminished clamor. "We had better hurry!" Kristin urged, picking up her pace toward the cave we saw from the kayak. "It looks too quiet. I hope we are still in time to get wine."

We were late. Did we miss our chance? Peering inside through an arched doorway big enough to admit a tractor, we saw the rough stone floor of the barn. The young man who managed the wine tastings was still there. He was packing up for the night, but he welcomed us in saying he would like to practice his English.

"I'm sorry, I won't open any more bottles today," he said as he worked. "My day is finished." I felt a twinge of regret, wishing we had arrived earlier. But as we chatted, he raised a dark green bottle to the light and shrugged.

"This was a particularly good red wine from here, and expensive. It is the last bottle we have, so you cannot buy any. If you would like to taste it anyway, you may. Otherwise I will pour it away."

His day may have finished, but he seemed in no hurry, asking us questions about our trip, about America, about England. He said he dreamed of traveling, but his family had made wine here for generations, and his life was here with the family wine. As we talked, he plied other leftovers on us, pouring away the remains from open bottles of wine he considered lesser quality, no matter how full, and selecting only the leftovers of the best for us to finish.

"I have to clear everything," he explained. "I need to be ready to start again fresh tomorrow. So have more if you like it. Here, try this one. It is also local."

Big Barges

In the end we left carrying two bottles of wine, wondering if we had already drunk a similar volume. The celebration was still in full swing as we weaved arm in arm through the crowd to mount the bridge for the view along the canal. From here we could see the canal narrow into the distance, from above instead of from the water.

This narrow, steep-arched, bridge was one of the original seventeenth century canal bridges, ridged with stony concrete underfoot. A new, cast bronze, plaque mounted on an adjacent wall, commemorated the friendship between United States and France. The name: Thomas Jefferson, curved around the top, followed by the respective dates commemorating independence: April 1789, and July 1828, flanking his relief. The date of installation was 2009, on the 220th anniversary of the French Revolution.

As we stood on the bridge, another large barge slowly approached. The nameplate read: *Alegria*: happiness, in Portuguese and Spanish. It sparked a memory of music in my head. *Alegrías* was one of the flamenco styles of guitar music I learned as a teenager, lively with a strict rhythmic structure.

Alegria, the barge, is one hundred feet long by sixteen feet wide. Like the *Alouette* it takes a maximum of four passengers. A week on board in 2021 will cost around $20,000. For the price of a fortnight onboard you could buy a new Tesla. A man lounged in the pool on deck, while a woman relaxed topless nearby, her knees offering some modesty as the boat slid slowly and carefully beneath our feet.

Back at our luxury kayak, Kristin slipped the wine bottles into the gaps alongside her seat, one each side. She had already discovered how each space there conveniently widened, although only just enough. Afterwards we always noticed a scuff or tear marking the wine label. The space beside the rear seat was too narrow for a bottle.

We did not paddle far from town before choosing a place to camp beside a vineyard. Nearby, a man quietly watered his field. It soon grew dark, and although the sounds of shouting, and dogs barking nearby, woke me occasionally, nothing prevented a good sleep.

Greeting the glow of dawn and a pleasant breeze, we savored the early morning golden sunlight as it first caught the treetops, and the far hill, and slowly climbed down toward us. The breeze rustled the reeds beneath the plane trees while our little espresso maker hissed and bubbled.

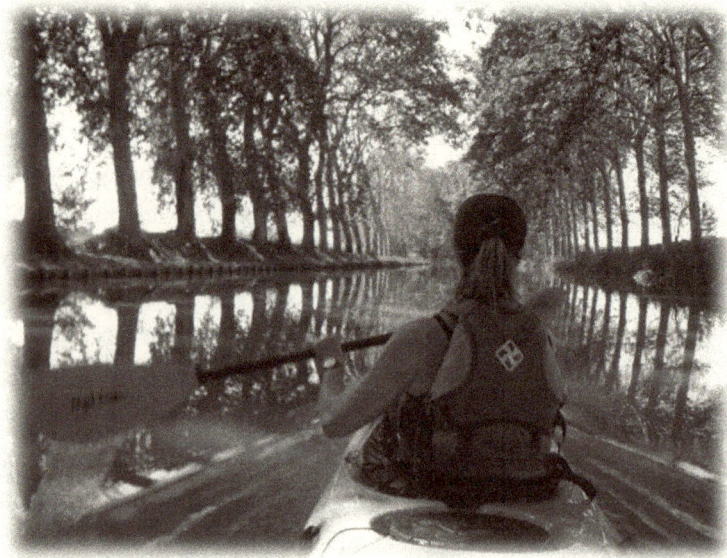

Avenue of plane trees.

10. Speckled by Rain

But that beginning was wiped out in fear
The day I swung suspended with the grapes,
And was come after like Eurydice
And brought down safely from the upper regions;
And the life I live now's an extra life
I can waste as I please on whom I please.[13]

It felt good to be paddling early, but early is not the best time for everything here. We glimpsed the long windows of a chateau above us, from the shade beneath a huge ancient plane tree, as we approached a bridge. We had reached Ventenac-en-Minervois, a town of about five hundred inhabitants. Beyond the bridge, a stone quay stood bathed in sunshine. The Chateau Ventenac-en-Minervois offered wine tours. But, to our disappointment, we discovered, they began at 10 am. We had arrived before nine.

The nineteenth century wine cave was in a tall, rectangular, building beneath a pitched clay-tiled roof. It adjoined a round tower with a conical slate turret. Adjacent stood shorter towers of greater diameter: huge wine fermentation vats of which I counted six.

Kayak across France

Ventenac-en-Minervois.

Mooring our kayak we explored. Between the bars of the tall, lock-and-chained, wrought iron gates we saw a garden that led uphill to a chateau facing the canal. Nowadays the wide building serves as a holiday residence, and kayaks lay incongruously beside the path in the landscaped garden.

Outside the boundary wall, we followed the quay to the *cave* at the end of the block: the building with a tower. Here was the entrance to the wine tours, if we were prepared to wait. Just along the quay was a kiosk selling newspapers, bread, wine, and sundry.

We should buy supplies, but first we climbed the steep hill beside the building, past a low-sided container. Rolled close to the wall, it collected the damp, maroon and purple, grape sludge that fell from a chute above. The heavy aroma of fermenting fruit filled the air around these grape solids, discarded from the must.

Farther up the hill stood another, blue, open-topped, trailer, this one filled with vine stems, ejected from a red-painted, metal, chute overhead. It felt cool and shaded in the narrow road, where the sun reflected the shapes of windows onto the crumbling stucco.

At the corner at the top of the hill, in a heavy arched stone gateway, massive wrought iron gates stood open to a yard. Two tractors stood parked: their trailers full of small dark grapes. Garnishing the grapes were green vine shoots, like those in the trailer at the side of the building.

These grapes were undoubtably picked by the machines we saw daily at work in the vineyards. The machines beat the vines to knock off the ripe grapes, but also break off some of the tender shoots. Although machines gather much of the harvest in the Languedoc-Roussillon region, around 20,000 seasonal workers are employed to hand pick grapes for some of the finer wines.

Dark grapes for winemaking.

Champagne production prohibits machine-harvesting. Nowadays, harvesting by hand requires some 100,000 seasonal pickers. At the time of year when Tim and I kayaked through the middle of the Champagne region, in March, there was nobody picking. But, coincidentally, Kristin, as a student, spent time hand-picked grapes there that same year, just a few months later.

Here at Ventenac-en-Minervois, harvested grapes come from the surrounding farms in trailers. Then, machinery separates the grapes from the green bits and banishes the greenery. It crushes the fruit into must for fermentation in the vats. After fermentation, filters take out the solids we saw ejected from the building. What about the wine? Well, we were too early to sample the end results at the wine tour.

We explored a little more before descending the steep hill to the kiosk, to buy a bottle of wine and some other supplies. The kiosk was safely a few meters out of range of the bottom of the hill. Nowadays, only a short section of wall and fence at the bottom of the hill would prevent a rolling car from ending up in the canal. But that wall is recent.

In the early days of the canal, horse-carts carried barrels of from the surrounding area to the canal for shipping. The carts descended this steep hill, to unload and stack the barrels on the quay to await a barge to Toulouse. The carts often ran out of control, losing barrels to the hill and to the canal at its end. So in the nineteenth century, building began on a new road: *Route Neuve*. This road, at a gentler incline, offered a safer route for the wine, and, more recently, a safe place for the kiosk.

Wines from the Languedoc region account for a third of all French wine production, and in 2001 the area of Languedoc-Roussillon produced more wine than the USA. It is the single biggest wine producing region in the world. The French classify most of the volume produced as *vin de table*, or table wine, which is the lowest wine classification. As such it is typically affordable as a *daily drinker*. However, Minervois AOC is one of the best-known appellations in Languedoc.

"Let's not wait for the tour," Kristin decided. "Otherwise it will be lunchtime before we get paddling again. I would enjoy a glass of wine more at the end of the day anyway."

I agreed. And we could always return to Ventenac-en-Minervois another year. I would expect to find people still making wine, just as they have ever since a former Roman soldier settled here in 300 AD and began growing vines.

So, we readied ourselves to paddle onward. As we drifted out onto the water, two black swans approached us. Sporting magnificent red beaks, and ruffled up feathers, the powerful birds cruised regally under no visible source of propulsion.

We paddled north, along a water corridor of reflected plane trees, between vineyards. A heady, fruity, fermenting aroma came from the fields where machines were harvesting grapes.

The canal here contours the side of the valley cut by the Répudre River. Limestone hills climbed to our right. But here and there beside the canal, lengths of brilliant orange mesh stretched from tree to tree. A sign alerted us. A fungal disease afflicts these plane trees, and it enters through points of damage. The notice requests that cyclists do not park cycles against them, boaters should not use them for mooring.

We soon reached the Répudre Aqueduct, the first aqueduct Riquet built on the Canal du Midi. Then, having crossed above the river Répudre, we began contouring south along the opposite side of the valley. When the contours on the map wiggle, so must the canal.

Turning west again we passed Paraza, a village spread up the hill to our right. Riquet stayed at the seventeenth century château here while constructing this part of the canal. There was a cluster of signs on the bank, advertising the chateau and other local businesses of interest to boaters. Most of the signs we passed along the canal related to wine. Shortly after Paraza we passed another village, Rubia, with another winery. We were truly in Languedoc wine country!

The wonderful light gradually clouded until we caught Pascal waiting at lock #56. We were just in time to ask him if he would tow our kayak through. Extra alert when the canal filled, I saw how the force of rushing water could easily push a boat sideways to damage the kayak. The weight would crack it like an egg. Pascal's team was efficient and careful, but another boat skipper sharing the space might not be as skilled. Locks were risky. One moment of someone else's inattention could easily put an end to our journey.

Also discouraging, the kayak snug alongside, I watched the bilge-pump spout dirty water straight into Kristin's cockpit. She resignedly sponged it all out before we boarded the kayak again.

Here, at Argens-Minervois, was as far as the French group would travel. A half mile, kilometer, beyond the lock they turned through one of the two entrances into a marina pool. A slipway, canal facilities, and a boat rental depot waited. Their canal trip was over. We felt sad to realize we would not run into them again in the coming days. Their exuberant energy had been uplifting.

Up on the hill, dominating the village, stood a partly ruined fourteenth century chateau with square towers. Curious, we took the opportunity to leave our camera batteries recharging at the marina while we investigated.

We climbed the road, which dead-ended at the chateau, our way blocked by the collapsed stonework of partly crumbled walls, and by the boarded doors and windows. A sign in French, hand-painted in green, prohibited entry. It also warned of the dangers of a fierce dog. This approach to the chateau was obviously not the usual entrance. There must be a main gate somewhere.

Less than a half mile to the north, hidden from where we sat beneath the chateau, is a large pond which feeds the canal via a creek. Everywhere here were waterways, ponds, and marshes. Man-made channels crisscross natural channels, all around.

From our vantage point, we could see the countryside spread across the valley. The sky was darkening, and I watched the weather close in on us. Even so we were in no hurry. At worst we would get wet.

Argens-Minervois.

Wandering back downhill, I stopped to investigate a stack of gnarled vine prunings, dark contorted sticks somehow tidily arranged against the wall. Beside the stack, on a tree that I suspected to be almond, hung leathery drupes. Some were splitting open on their twigs to reveal the characteristic hard shell inside. The nuts should be almost ready for harvest. September is when the drupes split open, but almonds ripen progressively from the top of the tree downward. Pickers must watch the top of the tree, harvesting from there first.

Back at the marina, we sat at a picnic table to enjoy the rest of last night's wine, while the sky, true to expectations, began spitting rain on us. Everyone else sought cover. The time had come for us to retrieve our camera batteries and move on.

While portaging the next lock we discovered that not everyone had taken shelter. A German couple in black hooded rain gear stood, gleaming wet. They stopped us to share hot coffee, from their flask, a touching kindness. Sipping, we stood talking with them for a few minutes. Random acts of kindness make memorable moments.

Raindrops now veiled the scene and speckled the water. Above us, the arching tree canopy crackled in the barrage. In the kayak, we stayed warm by paddling vigorously. Only at the portages did we become soaked and chilled, when we stood in the rain to lift the kayak and strap on the wheels ready to push uphill. I welcomed the coziness of the kayak after each portage.

At Homps, Kristin left the busy quay in search of supplies. Keeping an eye on the kayak, I joined some Canadians from Toronto who had stopped under cover on the quay for coffee. According to them, the restaurant-café we sheltered outside, *Café Peniche,* had a good reputation. The Canadians had rented a house to use as a base from which to explore by bicycle.

When a group of older French men stopped and stood over the kayak, I stepped back out into the rain to greet them. They were curious about the multiple hatches on the kayak, and the bag strapped onto the deck which resembled a gun case. Was it a gun? The name on the kayak reads; *DoubleShot.*

"No, it's just a spare paddle," I reassured, showing how our paddles took apart into two pieces.

"DoubleShot?"

"Espresso perhaps? Or maybe a little cognac?" I raised an imaginary glass to my lips and winked. They laughed. However, the bag often held more than just a spare paddle. It offered us a way to carry baguettes without crushing them.

Kristin now came bouncing back carrying cheese flans, fruit, and grapefruit juice. She also carried baguettes. Crouching, she slipped the baguettes into the paddle bag, and stowed everything else through a hatch. The men nodded knowingly to each other, and then wandered off.

The rain, pouring steadily, made us reluctant to stop to set up camp, so we decided to take a run at a couple more locks. Portaging one of them, Puichéric, we greeted a couple holding umbrellas against the rain. They were on vacation from Cambridge, England. "Did you come here to get away from the rain," I joked?

"Yes, it is a bit bleak today isn't it. Where are you two going in that?" He nodded toward our kayak on its wheels.

"Oh we're hiking from the Med to the Atlantic. But we are pulling that along behind us in case we want to paddle when we get there." When he looked at me and shook his head, I confessed, "Actually we're paddling from the Med' to the Atlantic, camping on the canal banks."

"Can you do that?" she asked.

"Yes! You just need to get a canal license. But the authorities prohibit kayaks from the locks, so we have to portage."

"We paddle a Canadian," she said. "It would be fun to try something like this." They looked at each other, considering the possibility.

"A canoe, Kristin. They paddle a canoe," I clarified as Kristin rolled her eyes. Then to the Brits I explained, "It has a different meaning in America, where a canoe is a canoe, a kayak is a kayak, a Canadian is someone from Canada, and paddling? Well, that is ambiguous."

We English commonly call the kayak a canoe, and the canoe a Canadian. It is one of the many examples of how the two nationalities, divided by a common language, misunderstand each other so well.

"Given all the portages we've made so far, we would have had an easier time in a canoe, with a couple of backpacks for our gear," I added.

It grew darker and extra shadowy, with showers of heavier rain between the partial shelter of the trees. The one cyclist we saw displaying a light showed up well, the stippled reflection in the canal as in winter on a wet road.

We saw many cyclists through the day, but few cyclists or barges toward evening. When day finally abandoned us, we chose the best location we could, on the right side between the canal and a road that ran above an overgrown embankment. We were beneath plane trees on bark-crunchy ground. We began clearing twigs and branches; debris that could poke us when we slept. We set aside a brick of sandstone and many, hard, round, plane seed balls, readying a large enough space for the tent.

Inside the cocooning cave we hung a headlamp. Beneath its glow, we were now ready to unfold a cloth onto the groundsheet, and to prepare a banquet of cheese, baguette, and fruit.

As owls hooted back and forth to each other in the trees above, Kristin savored her promised glass of wine.

11. Étang de Marseillette

Queer, with your thin wings
and your streaming legs
How you sail like a heron,
or a dull clot of air,
A nothingness.[14]

The Étang de Marseillette is an area of land, which used to be a brackish pond, more than three miles in diameter (5km). It formed some two million years ago, a leftover from the falling sea levels. The canal from here skirts the southern end of the étang. Just as the smaller Étang de Montady had caused sickness before the monks drained it in the fourteenth century, this one threatened with cholera, and mosquito-borne diseases.

Attempts to drain it in the sixteenth century by cutting a channel, the Canal Sud, and the Rigole de l'Étang, fed the water to the Aude River at Puichéric. Although this worked, the resulting marsh remained so salty that the land was still unfarmable. On the Canal du Midi, we would cross this drainage channel in a half mile from here.

The marsh remained unusable until, in 1851, workers dug a tunnel more than three miles long (5km), from farther upstream on the Aude River, to the marsh at Naudy. A new weir across the Aude held a head of fresh water which, via sluice, irrigated the marsh. The water still drained back into the Aude River downstream at Puichéric. Repeated freshwater floods, using this nineteenth century tunnel, flushed out the salt until the land became farmable. This newer tunnel also passes beneath the Canal du Midi.

I was fascinated by these saltwater marshes. Some, like the extensive one at Capestang, were an important source of salt, game, and fish. The draining of others helped to control diseases, and often created farmland. On topographical maps of the area, it is easy to spot the location of former étangs by the characteristic patterns of the fields and drainage. But many saltwater marshes, like this one, are at a higher elevation than I would have expected.

A string of lower elevation étangs once formed a continuous sheltered natural waterway, paralleling the coast of the Gulf of Lion from the Rhône to the Pyrenees. Over time, they have silted up in so many places, the old route is no longer navigable. Nowadays, canals fulfil the function, from the Rhône to as far as Narbonne, along much the same route.

Before weather forecasts, that natural waterway would have been a lifesaver. For in this corner of France two winds often blow ferociously offshore, the mistral, and the tramontane.

The mistral can blow at 40 miles per hour, upward to 115 miles per hour. It blows down the Rhône corridor, accelerated by the Venturi effect between the Massif Central and the Alps.

The tramontane begins when cool air from a high-pressure system on the Atlantic side, pours toward a low-pressure system on the Mediterranean side, in the Gulf of Lion. On the way, it accelerates between the Massif Central and the Pyrenees.

Both these winds blow offshore, powerfully and often abruptly. They sometimes combine. I have glimpsed their ferocity when kayaking on the south side of the Pyrenees, in Catalonia.

12. Carcassonne

They tell me, every day
not more or less than Sunday gay
In shining robes and garments fair
There people walk upon their way
One gazes there on castle walls
As grand as those of Babylon
A bishop and two generals!
I do not know fair Carcassonne,
I do not know fair Carcassonne![15]

An owl continued to be vocal in the morning as we made coffee, while a red squirrel made a racket right above our heads. Growing up in England, I developed a soft spot for red squirrels. There, illustrations of squirrels, in children's books, were typically of red squirrels. I adore their tufted ears and bushy tails. Smaller and already rarer than grey squirrels, I seldom ever saw one in England, so I was thrilled to be able to watch them here.

Back home in Seattle, grey squirrels are everywhere in the city, even finding a way into our attic one year to steal fiberglass insulation. In carrying it from bush to overhead wire along the road to their drey in the attic of another house, they left clues that helped us uncover what was going on. A trail of yellow fiberglass scraps caught in the bushes finally made that clear. Otherwise, the boisterous clatter of feet above our ceiling might have suggested the wily intruders had moved in.

At twice the size of a red squirrel, American grey squirrels, introduced into UK in the nineteenth century, soon became an invasive species. In most areas they have supplanted the shyer red squirrels.

But if my day began with memories of childhood books and woodland creatures, we soon reached a lock where the lockkeeper had left his own toys scattered around. Well, not exactly toys, but humorous sculptures in carved wood, or of welded metal. On display was a crudely carved, tall, and once-varnished, wooden sculpture of a man holding an acoustic guitar. Beside him stood a shorter figure, a metal sculpture of a man with long wirehair, playing a giant heavy metal electric guitar.

Over on the other side of the lock were a friendly pink pig and a flock of stiff wire-legged chickens. An animated wooden sculpture of a woman rode naked on a bicycle, wheels and legs spinning on the spot. A sculpture of a man, connected to a hose, his trousers open, peed water into a barrel.

I spotted more sculptures the longer I looked. One wooden man held up a wooden wine glass next to a sign that translated said: *To be thirsty for water is sad, but it must be said, to be thirsty for wine is twenty times worse.* I think this lockkeeper enjoyed his freedom of expression, also his wine.

We saw Trevor and Marilyn's boat where they had stopped near Trèbes and banged on the window. They told us they had planned to visit Carcassonne, but since it would involve something like nine more locks in each direction, it seemed too much. The weather forecast was for rain. It would get slippery; hazardous on the wet stonework for Marilyn who jumped ashore each time with the mooring lines. They decided to be sensible and safe, to take things easy and savor their remaining time afloat. We thanked them for all their help, and friendship, and wished them bon voyage.

Our route threaded between sandstone cliffs and steep slopes of mixed woodland, with brambles hung with ripe blackberries.

Many holidaymakers who book *le boat* rentals start at Trèbes, where we took a break for bread and pastries. Enough visitors come here to justify the tourist information center where we asked about Carcassonne.

"I recommend you stop well before you reach Carcassonne to camp," the assistant advised. "It will not be easy to find somewhere when you get closer. But when you arrive, you will find a harbormaster on the left bank who can help you if you stop during the day to visit the town."

We thanked him for his help. It would be eight miles before we reached the marina at Carcassonne. We could surely find somewhere to camp before then.

Soon after, tucked comfortably in our tent among bushes beneath the trees, we sheltered from the rain that Trevor had accurately forecast. From there we hailed a small yacht, without a mast, waving to it as it passed slowly under motor. Any sailboat was a rare sight on the canal. As such, I felt kinship with it, a fellow oddity on the canal. But now in the growing dark, the skipper sitting in waterproofs in the cockpit did not see us. His engine must have drowned our calls of greeting. The boat was the *Patte Blue.*

Next morning, intending to have as much time exploring Carcassonne as possible, we left our comfortable spot before breakfast. We dressed in our best clothes beneath our waterproofs, planning to stop at the first lock for breakfast. When we arrived, the little *Patte Blue* waited at the bank for the lockkeeper to begin his day. The owner, Jean Pierre, invited us on board for coffee.

Sheltering in the cozy cabin sat his wife, Bettie. We asked where they came from.

"Perpignan," he replied. "We live on a saltwater lagoon nearby."

Perpignan is some eighty miles along the coast south of Narbonne, so I asked, "Did you come up the canal de Robine?"

"No," he said regretfully. "That is a beautiful canal, but it is too shallow: our keel is too deep. We had to go around the long way."

That meant another twenty-five miles of open coast to navigate from Perpignan before the next possible entrance at Agde. Since that entrance led to the Canal du Midi at the round lock, I hinted to them of my earlier mistake.

"We came from Sète, but we nearly paddled down that canal from the round lock."

He looked questioningly, so I confessed.

"We took a wrong turn…" Out came the whole story.

He laughed, and then in jest, with an expression of astonishment, "You have no GPS?"

"No, but we have used a compass ever since," I countered, also tongue in cheek. He laughed again. "I was in disbelief at what had happened!" Then I asked, "What does *Patte Blue* mean? Blue what?"

Jean Pierre explained how *Patte* means paw, in reference to what English sailors would call a *cat's paw*, the ruffled surface on the water caused by a light gust of wind.

JP and Bettie planned to go just as far as Carcassonne, to see the town: the dream of the farmer in Gustave Nadaud's nineteenth century chanson: *Carcassonne.*

Carcassonne sits at a bend in the Aude River. The river, having flowed north from the Pyrenees, meets its tributary the Fresquel a half mile from here, a kilometer. From there, the Aude turns east toward Narbonne. The canal du Midi, which originally followed the Fresquel upstream, takes a sharp turn south instead, rerouted through Carcassonne.

Carcassonne

Although the townspeople of Carcassonne wanted the canal to go through the town, it did not do so until after the French Revolutionary wars. Completion of the new route in 1810 took advantage of the manual labor of thousands of Austrian and Prussian prisoners of war. The new route started just here, where the lock gates at last opened permitting *Patte Blue* to enter the first of the series of locks.

With no need to wait, we carried around those, and another lock shortly after, and forged ahead into the town. Just as the tourist information guide had cautioned, we saw no place where we might have camped.

Portaging the town lock, we relaunched over an awkward stone quay into the boat basin. At the canal service area, the harbormaster kindly helped us haul the kayak onto the end of a wooden dock. Finding marina facilities available, we showered ready for town.

Our first tour stop was the cemetery, a few hundred yards walk to the north, in the opposite direction from the old town. It stood on a hill from which we could view the old walled town. Carcassonne, looking like a fairytale castle, stood on its own hill across the Aude valley. It is easier to grasp the extent of a town from a distance than from inside.

Stretched above the cemetery gates, and on some of the gravestones, were carvings and reliefs of large bats, wings outspread. It seemed odd to me, conjuring creepy scenes of nighttime in the cemetery, unseen movements in the darkness, the air alive with the leathery sound of wings and high-pitched squeaking calls. Were these carvings of the creatures of the night here to warn people away?

Dispassionately, a graveyard is the perfect place for bats, with places to hide and plenty to forage. That might account for why in some cultures, bats symbolize rebirth. Bats emerge from mother earth each night, issuing from cemeteries as if the dead were being reborn. But reborn into what form? Into something like Bram Stoker's Dracula?

Fortified Town of Carcassonne.

Having seen the distant view of the walled town, we hurried to reach the open market. I was glad we were quick, for many stall keepers were already packing up ready for the market to close at midday. They had stacked crates ready to carry away, and left piles of discarded packaging, and a few broken melons. We would have been too late had we delayed any longer.

The market was situated in the Bastide Saint Louis, across the river Aude from the walled town. Once surrounded by a defensive moat, the design of the bastide was what had become the typical square grid street pattern around a central square. Place Carnot, with the open market, is that central square,

The bastide is more recent than the walled town. At the start of the Albigensian crusade in 1209, the inhabitants of Carcassonne must have been fully aware of the fate of those at Béziers when a few days later they found themselves under siege. At Béziers, after the slaughter, the attackers looted and then burned the town.

But since an intact town would be more valuable than another smoking ruin, the attackers laying siege to Carcassonne offered free exit to the inhabitants if they left everything behind. When the townspeople accepted that alternative, the attackers upheld their bargain, although I doubt the Cathars could live with their religion for long after that, with the inquisition following the crusade. The victors at once began to build stronger defenses around the town.

In 1260, following the Albigensian crusade, the townspeople ejected from Carcassonne built a new town, the Bastide Saint Louis, across the river. The Aude region built many of these planned villages, bastides, following a treaty with France in 1229. Languedoc was becoming part of France and life was beginning to recover following the demise of the Cathars. Bastides offered a new type of economic center which reduced the power of the local lords, since farmers moving to the new settlements became freemen.

The new, lower, town had poor defenses compared to the old one. In 1355 during the hundred years war, when the English Black Prince destroyed the Bastide Saint Louis, he found the old town too well defended, and so moved on.

The bastide, rebuilt, prospered on textile manufacturing. By the seventeenth century, on completion of the Canal du Midi, and into the eighteenth century, many wealthy merchants lived in Bastide Saint Louis in grand houses. Despite their influence, the canal bypassed the town until the nineteenth century.

The canal basin of the rerouted canal, where we left our kayak, is at the northern border of the Bastide Saint Louis. Grand boulevards which delineate the old bastide, have replaced the remaining moats, although the town has long since spread wide.

A spectacular twelve-arched bridge crosses the river Aude. It links the two towns, known collectively as Carcassonne. We crossed it to begin the humbling approach beneath the watchful battlements, up the hill toward the gates.

The walled town's impressive construction, a ditch and rampart surrounding two curtain walls, watch towers and a broad space between, is recent, as compared to its overall history. When Carcassonne fell to Simon de Montfort and the catholic crusaders in 1209, a single curtain wall, overlooked by the citadel, surrounded the town. The victors built the second, outer wall, and soon fifty-two defensive towers stood guarding the walls. These new defenses later proved sufficient to fend off the Black Prince.

It is easy to assume that the fortifications have looked the same ever since. But restoration in the nineteenth century brought a more northern sensibility. Steep slate roofs on the towers replaced the flatter roofs under clay tiles more typical here.

I saw clues to the older heritage of some of the towers around the lower parts, where bands of thin, red, Roman bricks, and stone remained. The lower sections of some of the older walls stand inside the newer walls. Some of the old towers with red brick lean from vertical. I hope they are stable since the restored towers stand upright on top of the leaning parts.

The Romans built fortifications here long before the Middle Ages, but a Celtic oppidum predates even them. This, established earlier than the oppidum at Ensérune, dated as far back as 3,500 BC.

Passing through the second ring-wall gate, we reached a bustling town of tightly packed buildings, pantile roofs and narrow cobbled streets. The old town caters to tourists. Shops sell souvenirs such as plastic swords, shields, and armor. Printed dishcloths and t-shirts are for sale, and cafés and restaurants beckon to the weary and hungry.

Carcassonne

Gateway into Carcassonne.

We explored the citadel, the castle within the fortified town, and toured the towers and halls all around the town. Altered, or not, through the centuries, the structure I saw today impressed me.

Inside the inner walls we see today, the gothic Roman Catholic Basilica of Saints Nazaire-et-Celse, of the late thirteenth century, stands tall. Long, narrow, stained-glass windows illuminate its interior. The vastness of the enclosed space dwarfs even the huge pipe organ.

The basilica stands where the Visigoths founded a church in the sixth century, before the Saracens took the town in 725. The church, like the town, has a multi-layered past.

Then we continued around the ramparts, looking out over the orange roofs of the lower town and in the other direction across to the Pyrenees.

"Ice cream?" tempted Kristin.

I needed no second invitation to stop, but alert to details while waiting in line, I remarked, "Have you noticed the cobbled streets?" Of course she had. "And so, have you noticed how many well-dressed women are running all over them in high heels? With never a misstep? I am sure that takes a lot of practice!"

We found *Patte Blue* moored close by our kayak. JP and Bettie were relaxing on board and readily spent a little more time chatting with us before we left.

Soon out of town into farmland we found a quiet spot to camp. Regiments of vines lined the field across the canal, yet it felt like open country, free from human touch.

In the chilly evening, we enjoyed Minervois wine, leek flan, and Roquefort flan, to finish with a little Cognac. We may not have been the only ones having a little tipple with dinner. Nearby, English holidaymakers were enjoying themselves on board two barges. They sounded well lubricated, partying loudly all night, their happiness ringing out across the countryside.

13. Bram

He drew a circle that shut me out
Heretic, rebel, a thing to flout.
But love and I had the wit to win:
We drew a circle and took him in![16]

Bram lies about fourteen canal miles from Carcassonne, a mile's walk from the canal. Its pattern of concentric circles on the map first caught my eye. Was the old part of the town planned like that for defensive purposes, I wondered?

A settlement with streets in concentric circles, like Bram, is a *circulade*. Historians have recently made a distinction between these, and the many bastides in the Aude region built following the Albigensian crusade. Bastides usually had a rectangular grid pattern around an often-arcaded market square. The church is usually set to one side of the center. Those villages planned on a circular pattern are usually older than rectangular bastides.

Bram supported Catharism and in 1210 resisted attacks by Crusaders. When the town fell after three days, Simon de Montfort brutally punished his prisoners by cutting away the upper lip and nose and gouging out the eyes of all but one, who he left with one eye. He then sent these faceless people, one hundred of them, away to the Cathar stronghold at the castle of Lastours, fifteen miles away, as a warning. Each sightless person held the shoulder of the one ahead, the one-eyed man leading.

Carved stonework beside church door, Bram.

What fortifications guarded Bram, before Simon de Montfort arrived, is unclear. The Roman town, Eburomagus, existed on the site in 60 BC, on the south side of the preexisting Via Aquitania. This then well-traveled road, passing here as the minor route D33, came from Narbonne via Carcassonne on its way toward Castelnaudary and beyond, along the same route we followed. I assume the Romans built Eburomagus, as a fort, according to a standard rectangular planned layout.

The current town, in its pattern of concentric circles, is from a late as the eleventh century. The designer could mark the first circle using a central post and a rope, to position a wall surrounded by a moat. I have read that there was only one entrance, toward the east. Nowadays there are several.

Houses would have stood against the inside of the wall and there may have been a castle tower in the center. There has been a church at the center ever since the Albigensian crusade, but there is no reference to one before. As the settlement grew, each new concentric circle of houses needed fortification around the outside.

Our approach to town was via a wide footpath which ran beside a road, an avenue of plane trees. On either side were broad, dry, level, fields under stubble left from the grain harvest. In contrast, Bram conferred an almost stifling sense of confinement within its narrow, cambered curving streets. Between the pale wash-colored houses, the roads curved so tightly we could not always see the next street junction, just a few yards away. Although nowadays there are three radial roads, we eased toward the center as if negotiating a maze.

Shallow-pitched, clay-tiled, roofs capped narrow houses two or three storeys high. Wooden shutters hung open, above a shoulder width of sidewalk just wide enough to accommodate a step down from front door to street. An armful of pink petunias bursting from a terracotta pot beside a door completely blocked the sidewalk. Hollyhocks reached tall against a wall. Overhead hung pots of red geraniums within watering reach of an upstairs window.

Curving street, Bram.

At the center of the town stood the buttressed fort-like tower of the Saint Julien church. In the cramped space around, I could barely step back far enough to appreciate its style or extent. Like most churches, it must always be under modification and repair, and there will have been many changes since the first reference to a church here in 1210,

We unwound through the streets, circling from the tight curves into more open ones to reach the edge of the village. From there, the straight line of plane trees, each tree with a hand on the shoulder of the one in front, led us back to the canal.

Lockkeepers on the Canal du Midi are people of personality. Leaving Bram, we passed three locks to Villepinte-Aude and then two beyond. Slowing toward a third, we scouted for the easiest place to slide the kayak from the canal. Having heaved it ashore, I assembled the trolley, reaching down into my cockpit for the wheels and clipping them onto the frame. Pushing uphill, we came upon a tranquil setting: lockkeepers at ease.

A man and woman sat relaxing, glasses of wine beside them on a small table against the wall of the lockkeeper's cottage. The warm evening sun cast long shadows. We greeted, noticing a sign that offered preserves and ceramics and a few items of food for sale.

La boutique de l'écluse, I read as we stepped into the side room to browse, selecting a few items such as pâté and wine.

Now we learned that Frederika, who had left her table to join us inside, was the ceramicist who made the colorful little souvenir tiles for sale, depicting the lock and the lockkeeper's cottage.

"Kristin makes ceramics too," I boasted.

"But bowls and vases. It's different," Kristin murmured dismissively under her breath, not wanting me to mention it.

Frederika's husband, Jean Louis, was a writer. They were both enjoying their stay here.

Stowing our small purchase, we said goodbye, found a suitable stretch of bank and slid the kayak sideways onto the water. But as it splashed down, Kristin cried out, "Oh no! the *pochette*! It fell off the deck. I didn't clip it on."

"Well, it can't have gone far. It must be just around here where we launched. It should float."

The *pochette* was the small waterproof bag in which we carried our cash. Kristin typically kept it handy, clipped onto the deck lines in front of her. It held our money, including coins, and items like my penknife. The clear-plastic window of the bag's side-pocket held our canal license ready to show. Since we could not find it, the contents must have been heavy enough to sink the bag.

The water in the canal was dirty, and we could not see down. "It was my fault," Kristin admitted. "I was careless. I'll see if I can feel it with my feet."

"Are you sure? That might not be smart."

But she took off her shoes and waded cautiously in, then almost lost her balance.

"Be careful," I warned, "You might find broken glass."

"Nigel, float the kayak to me. I cannot tell how deep it gets. I need something to hold onto. Was it over here more? Ugh! This mud feels icky!"

The canal was not very deep. Even some feet from shore the water only reached to Kristin's chest. Dense grey swirls of sediment, stirred up from the bottom, now clouded the surface. Kristin could not feel the bag.

Frederika, now walking her dog, hurried toward us. "It is not good to be in the canal!" She scolded. "The water is dirty. You catch a disease, leptospirosis." She turned to me imploring, "You must help get her out!"

In fact swimming is prohibited in the Canal du Midi, and Kristin came perilously close to breaking that rule. Another couple out walking stopped to ask what was going on.

"We dropped our bag in the water somewhere here. We are trying to find it."

"You should use a rake. Can you borrow one? Try that house. See if anyone is at home."

"I live there," Frederika butted in, "and yes, I do have one. I'll go." She headed for the house and returned carrying two rakes, passing one to Kristin. As Kristin leaned on the kayak to take it, the kayak dipped toward her. Up from the other side bounced the bag. Somehow it must have washed underneath the kayak when we launched, and then got stuck, its flotation holding it up against the hull despite all the swinging around.

Frederika insisted Kristin follow her into the house. "You must shower. That water is not good. Come on, I have towels."

So we hauled the kayak back on land and Frederika bustled Kristin inside.

Bram

As I stood in the evening sun, Jean Louis called out, "Come sit down." He gestured toward the table where he and Frederika sat when we first arrived. I realized with shame how we had interrupted their evening. Their glasses were not yet empty.

"I'll bring more wine," Jean Louis decided, slipping indoors for a few moments. He reappeared carrying another bottle of wine and more glasses. He went back for cheese and bread.

By the time Kristin and Frederika joined us, the level of wine in the bottle was lower, with the sun correspondingly close to vanishing beyond the horizon.

"It's too late to be on the canal," they insisted. "You can camp tonight in our garden if you like. Best take your kayak with you, just in case." They were generous in making it convenient for us.

We rejoined them, as soon as our tent was ready, and sat chatting beyond the twilight. Snacking on pâté and cheeses, slices of apple and pear, and bread and wine, we lingered until the bright moon flew high above the plane trees.

Our garden site was comfortable, although the cloudless sky brought a chill to the night. I still felt that crispness when Kristin slipped out from the sleeping bag into the early morning. Cozied down, I could soon hear the stove, and then the hiss of the espresso maker. Kristin passed a little ceramic cup of coffee into the tent for me, with a smile, and then vanished. I assumed she had left to take photos in the special light of morning. She was adept at capturing those moments. She seemed to be gone for a long time.

The DoubleShot parked beside the house.

I discovered where she had gone when I got up. She was poking at the garden hedge, trying to burrow a way out through it. She explained how she threw the spent coffee grounds through the hedge and accidentally flung the stainless-steel filter too. She could not find it. In the end I walked along the canal until I found a gate to the field behind the garden. Kristin guided me to the location from the other side of the hedge.

After a little searching, I spotted the filter at the foot of the hedge. It hung, caught in the grasses, suspended precariously above a water-filled ditch. I balanced carefully, reaching my paddle across the ditch, and jiggled the filter onto the blade. Cautiously I brought the little escapee back across the water into captivity.

Our stop had offered us the most delightful company and the strangest of challenges, events we would laugh about every time we saw our little souvenir tile.

Bram

Castelnaudary was not far away, but steeply uphill past single, double, triple, and quadruple flights of locks. Flights of multiple locks were always arduous work, leaving us drained yet relieved when we reached the top. We looked forward to arriving at the town and taking a break.

Castelnaudary is a market town midway between Toulouse and the Mediterranean. It stands on the site of the Roman town, Sostomagus, on the Via Aquitania. The canal du Midi helped Castelnaudary become prosperous as a major canal port.

It felt wonderful to exit the canal to see a wide expanse of water, the wind blowing at our face, the waves crackling against the hull. This sizeable pool, the *Grand Bassin*, holds enough water to supply the locks we had toiled beside. A holiday barge cruised across the pool toward us, six men and women on deck, bundled to keep warm, looking furtively all around them as if unsure of the depth, blue fenders dragging and bouncing against the water.

Looking back: The pool at Castelnaudary.

At the far end of the lake, the narrow gap beneath a tall stone bridge signaled where the route squeezes for a moment before widening to the port quay. The port quay is the Castelnaudary dockside. There, during the canal's commercial heyday, carters brought locally grown produce and crafted goods for loading onto barges bound for Toulouse or the Mediterranean and carried away offloaded goods.

The town covers the hill behind the pool. We soon found ourselves scaling the streets to the churches at the top, the spires of which are visible from far around.

People often associate Castelnaudary with cassoulet. A cassoulet is a stew typically prepared from white beans. With pork, duck, or goose, or a combination of those meats, everything cooks together for a long time. It is a Languedoc speciality, with many variations. The Castelnaudary version usually features goose or duck confit, pork shoulder and sausage with white lingot beans. During its long cooking, the crust which develops and browns on top is from time to time broken up and stirred in, adding to the final texture.

The name of the dish, cassoulet, is from the cassole, an earthenware bowl. Glazed inside, the cassole is for slow cooking. An Italian potter made such bowls at Issel, a small circulade about three miles north, (5km). He set up shop there in 1377, and potters have continued to make cassoles there ever since.

That was almost two hundred years before Catherine de' Medici received lingot or haricot beans, a cultivar of *Paseolus vulgaris,* as a wedding gift in 1533. The beans were one of several exotic plants brought back from the Americas following Columbus's voyages. Catherine then encouraged people in the region between Carcassonne and Toulouse to grow lingot beans, where they became the basis for the new dish: cassoulet.

Cyclists on the towpath.

We sat on a wall to sip wine from our tiny ceramic cups, before rejoining the canal, heading from town into the tree-lined corridors that wind past vineyards and fields of sunflowers. The fields must have been spectacular in bloom, but by now the leaves and petals were brown, with the bowed seed heads ripening. Hills textured the background. Canal-side cyclists passed, silhouetted against the sky.

About five miles beyond Castelnaudary is the so-called Mediterranean lock, above which is the highest section of the Canal du Midi. Just before that lock, on the left, is a pottery that appears to contradict itself: the *Pottery Not*. The pottery owners, in what I believe to be another contradiction, are the Not brothers. They throw clay, dug from their back yard, hand-shaping bowls and cassoles on their spinning potters' wheels.

Once the pottery has dried, the brothers bisque-bake it in a wood-fired kiln, before gloss-glazing the inside of each item. They fire the pottery a second time to waterproof the natural terracotta by melting that gloss glaze. The resulting gloss is in luscious green, yellow, white, or French blue, or is simply ice clear, appearing gleaming wet as if freshly poured across the natural terracotta color.

Rooftop sculpture at the Not Pottery.

The Not brothers, who are brothers, at the Not pottery, which is a pottery, are famous for their cassoles. Their grandfather began digging clay and firing pottery here beside the canal in the nineteenth century, and the business has continued through the generations. Here they honor a profession that has thrived in the Aude for more than two thousand years.

"Longer than that," Kristin commented. "People have been making pottery forever. It's probably the world's second oldest profession."

We slid the kayak from the water and assembled the trolly. As I lifted one end high to allow Kristin to position it underneath, I reminded her joyfully, "Finally, the last uphill push! After this it is downhill all the way to the Atlantic." I lowered the kayak carefully onto the wheels and stepped away, straightening my back.

The loaded tandem was heavy. Lifting even one end to hold up at head height, so Kristin could position the trolly, was heavy work. I felt the twinges in my back every time. The trolly, too, bowed to the weight. Over the days uphill, the wheels gradually splayed apart, angling wider at the ground. The change was slow but steady.

With the wheels strapped in place, we each took an end of the kayak, one pulling the other pushing, building speed, running along the gravel to tackle the steep incline.

Beyond each lock we reversed the process. We unstrapped the trolly and I lifted the kayak again to let Kristin slide the wheels away. Choosing a place cushioned with vegetation, we slid the kayak through the grasses and wildflowers onto the water.

Happy to have reached the highest section of the canal, we now scouted for a place to camp. We soon found somewhere. A tree had fallen into the water, reshaping the bank into an easy harbor landing, on the bend before the village, Le Ségala.

I set to, carefully trimming a few tiny briars and thorny roses before pitching the tent. A steep rise behind us sheltered the tent from the wind. This wind, having kicked up through the afternoon as the sky clouded, now rushed through the trees with the roar of heavy surf.

Across the canal, beyond a field, lights glowed either from the road, or from railway signals. On our side of the canal, beyond the rise and a thicket of trees, lay ploughed fields, farms, and the pantiled roofs of a tight cluster houses. This settlement, Labastide-d'Angou, founded in 1373, was one of the last bastides established in the area.

Labastide-d'Angou was rectilinear. Historians accept that the earliest bastides date from the thirteenth century, replacing villages destroyed in the Albigensian crusade. However, some consider a few to be earlier, from the twelfth century. The 1229 Treaty of Paris forbade the fortification of bastides, yet inhabitants often built defenses later. Labastide-d'Angou had fortifications. The Black Prince had destroyed the Bastide Saint Louis at Carcassonne just eighteen years earlier. Some form of defense here must have seemed prudent.

I was beginning to get a sense of how people and events had reshaped the countryside around here. The Albigensian crusade and the inquisition that followed brought about a lot of change. But afterwards came the hundred years' war between England and France, from 1337 to 1453. In that time, the Black Prince's chevauchées crossed Languedoc from English-held Bordeaux, ravaging the countryside, villages, and towns as far as Narbonne. People rebuilt their settlements following each catastrophe, only to see their homes plundered and burned once more. It is no wonder that so many settlements, no matter how small, were fortified.

14. Parting of the Waters

Toad to Ratty: "You surely don't mean to stick to your dull fusty old river all your life, and just live in a hole in a bank, and BOAT? I want to show you the world!"[17]

Riquet's Canal du Midi is a summit canal. That is, it connects between the heads of two valleys, as opposed to a lateral canal which runs down a river valley. A lateral canal can take water from the river it follows to supply its topmost locks, but that is not possible where a canal crosses a watershed. Since water leaves the highest section every time a vessel enters or exits it, finding a way to replace that water here, at the top, was key to the operation of Riquet's canal. He had to find a water supply.

His solution was to build a dam on higher land to the northeast, at the edge of the Black Mountains, the southwestern end of the Massif Central, to create a reservoir. From this reservoir near the town of Revel, he channeled water along a feeder canal for about twenty-five miles to the summit section of the Canal du Midi.

From there, the water goes downhill either to the Mediterranean or to the Atlantic, depending on which lock it enters. For that reason, the place where the feeder canal enters the Canal du Midi is known as *the parting of the waters*.

The summit section of canal is at 650 feet above sea level (189m). We pushed through a thin layer of brown and golden colored tree leaves that littered the water, which made the day seem more like autumn than late summer. How much of that change was due to elevation, and how much to the changing season, I wondered? Might we see a difference, leaving the valley on the Mediterranean side for the one falling to the Atlantic?

A boat passed us before we launched in the morning, not something that happened often. Boats seldom moved outside the hours of lock operation, which ran from nine in the morning until seven in the evening. Since we always paddled until late, boats rarely passed our camp unless we were late rising in the morning.

La Ségala looked as sleepy as we felt passing it. Kristin admired the colorful shutters, and drew my attention to the pastel green, French blue, and navy, which brightened the houses on the left bank. Soon we arrived at the parting of the waters.

A cast-metal commemorative plaque on our right showed the distances to different elements of the water supply system. We landed beside the channel where water enters the canal, and followed it upstream, past a sluice to the place intended by Riquet as a holding pond for the canal. His pond did not function as expected, and soon silted up. Abandoned in 1750, only an octagonal channel of water remains, as a border to a grassy field where the pond once lay. An avenue of plane trees ran across the field. Having skirted the octagon, we could see how the trees, standing tall, arched above a narrow gravel path.

A little farther up the hill stood a tall obelisk on a hillock or rocky mound, a tribute to Riquet. The mound, surrounded by a circular wall, guarded by cast iron gates, stands within a ring of tall conifers. All told, the monument exerts a fort-like presence.

Although we could not enter the locked gates, here was a good viewpoint, looking out across rolling hills of farmland. Yellow leaves cloaked the ground around the deciduous trees, even though the leaves still on the trees were green. Again it felt like an omen of autumn on its way. Especially so, when despite the appearance of a brightening sky, rain splattered down.

Memorial to Riquet at Parting of Waters.

I found it easy to dally. The chuckling water from the Black Mountains passes a mill on its way to the canal, tempting me to explore upstream. But instead we returned, walking the length of the shady plane avenue, to find walnut trees at the far end. Walnuts littered the ground. Easy to crack, the nuts tasted fresh and buttery. We followed the path, as far as the first lock on the Atlantic side, before backtracking to our kayak to resume our journey.

Our journey would now be downstream, but downstream is a misleading term. The only downhill parts that made any difference to us were the portages. We still lifted and wheeled, but now we had to hold the kayak back from running away down the steep slopes.

Avenue of plane trees at the parting of the waters.

With each portage, our wheels seemed to spread ever wider. The upper part of the tyres leaned inward so much they rubbed against the straps and the hull of the kayak. I began to worry, for although we had passed the point of highest elevation, we would negotiate as many locks on our way down to the Atlantic as we had on our ascent.

Parting of the Waters

We relied on our wheels to portage, but we had two other options. To carry around, we would have to unload the kayak at each lock, making several journeys on foot to ferry everything. That would be tedious and time-consuming. Otherwise we must find a way to stay afloat. To lessen the burden on the wheels, we once more tried the latter.

At a double lock, we asked the lockkeeper, Jacque, if he would let us line our kayak through. He looked at us calmly and agreed. Wearing his black hair cut short, and a dark stubble shadow, smart navy trousers and crisp t-shirt, he watched as the water drained from the lock. He appeared mildly amused by me feeding out line as our kayak disappeared into the void.

It being a double lock, Jacque encouraged us to get into our kayak before he emptied the second. It would be easier he said. Lining the kayak out from the lock afterward to a suitable place to embark would be awkward. I wished all lockkeepers were as helpful.

It was later, while portaging a double lock at Sanglier, that the metal frame of the trolly gave up and broke. I was crestfallen. What could we do?

Kristin phoned Richard of Point65. Since we were without a phone data plan and had no Wi-Fi available, he kindly offered to search for a trolly online.

"What is the mailing address where you are at?" he asked.

"I don't know. I'll see if we can find someone to ask," Kristin said, but there was nobody around. This late, the lockkeeper had gone home. Hoping we would have more success at the next lock, we manhandled our kayak to the water and then sprinted the mile to écluse d'Ayguesvives. Again we searched for a lockkeeper without success.

A young lady who saw us looking asked if she could help, and we explained our predicament.

"Your friend can mail the wheels to me if you like. I can drive them to you when they arrive. Would you like me to talk to him? By the way, my name is Luce." We introduced ourselves.

When we called Richard back, he and Luce conversed in French to make the arrangements. Then, with daylight fading, we chose to stay there overnight. According to Luce, the lockkeeper would not return until morning. Expecting to leave early, we set the tent nearby on a rise above a cycleway, the shortest distance to carry the kayak.

We had found a visually attractive but unfortunately noisy location, for a main road ran over a bridge behind the trees just beyond the lock, and roads ran nearby to either side. Besides awaking at the sounds of cars and trains, we awoke to find anglers clumping around at three in the morning. It was light, and the fat full moon shone so brightly through the tent fabric, it deceived me into thinking it was sunlight.

Our camping spot was not the ideal place to stay to wait for new wheels; we preferred more secluded locations. And since we were right in the middle between seas, we must keep going if we were to reach the Atlantic before running out of time. Keeping those criteria in mind, we got up at first light to make coffee and breakfast on the dew-damp grass. A cockerel crowed loudly nearby, and cyclists sped by along the path.

"I think we should wait for the lockkeeper and ask him to let us through." Kristin suggested.

"They don't usually let us. Why would they here?"

"If I explain about the wheels, why would he not be reasonable? The other one, Jacque, let us through yesterday."

"I think we should carry around and load the kayak below the lock. That way, independent, we can leave as soon as we are ready."

Kristin prevailed. We waited, and just as she had predicted, the lockkeeper let us into the lock. Dark damp walls slid from the water beside us as we dropped, swallowing us in gloom. As the gates opened, we waved our thanks and paddled out to see Jacques, from yesterday, standing watching from the road bridge above. For a reason we could not understand, and he was unable to explain, Luce had asked him to meet us. In the end, faltering in the face of our inadequate French, he waved us on.

At the next lock we found Luce, standing beside Jacque, happy to see us. Only now we discovered they were both lockkeepers.

Luce explained, "Your friend Richard has found wheels for you. It is Jacque's day off. He will drive you to where you can buy them. Jacque smiled awkwardly. He must have come ready to take us, meeting us earlier but unable to explain why.

I sat beside him in his little car as we sped along the country lanes, through villages and past ancient churches. Our destination, a Decathlon store at Portet-sur-Garonne, was some ten miles away on the outskirts of Toulouse. Arriving, we entered the vast warehouse of sports equipment, marveling at the variety of goods for all sports. Despite it being a sports equipment store, I felt strangely out of place wearing my plastic clogs, t-shirt, and shorts.

Richard had reserved the trolly and wheels for us, and a lively shop assistant fetched them. Leaving with exactly what we needed, I felt wonderfully relieved. Soon we were on our way back, zipping along the twisting lanes toward the canal.

Jacque pointed out the gleaming new cancer research buildings, then the brick walls that hid the old factory where Airbus built planes early in its history. Here and there stood wall-tower churches, a characteristic of the region. Silhouetted in gaps in the high walls that serve as towers were rows of hanging bells.

Jacque, noticeably more relaxed, chatted confidently. His English was more fluent than my French. Although I understand quite a lot, my spoken French is pitiful. When talking I pause, trying to formulate the grammar correctly, before I speak, so the conversation stalls. Kristin on the other hand blurts out a stream of conversation in *Franglais* and everything flows along just fine.

Kristin and Luce, chatting together, were glad to see we had found the new wheels. We assembled them and compared them, gleaming new and clean, beside the well-worn and broken set. Then Luce invited us to join her for lunch on the grass. Sitting beneath a tree, she shared her poulet stew which was hearty and delicious.

"My husband made it," she smiled when I complimented her cooking. "He is an Arab. He knows how to make food taste good!"

After lunch, it was Luce who operated the lock for us to pass, before we waved a fond farewell to her, and to Jacque. Kindly aided by Richard, Luce, and Jacque, we were on our way again having lost no more than a few hours. We felt extremely fortunate.

Our luck held at the next lock too, where the lockkeeper, a young woman, let us through. But at the following one, canal officials stood on board a barge that maneuvered slowly, blocking our way. A camera mounted on a long arm reached out from it over the water.

The friendly camera crew said they were making a film to promote the canal. The lock gates stood open, welcoming, but the officials on board arrogantly berated us, telling us how kayaks were forbidden, and that we must carry around. They made a big deal of it as they entered the lock.

We portaged, but by the time we reached the other end, the barge had already left the lock and now blocked the only launch spot suitable for a kayak. From the officious manner of the men on the barge, we suspected it had been deliberate. Not wishing to appear inconvenienced, we simply launched, albeit awkwardly, farther down.

We were approaching Toulouse. Many more boats and barges sat moored along the canal here. Uncertain how we would fare getting through town, we stopped at Port Sud marina to seek advice at the harbormaster's office. The harbormaster recommended stopping at Port Saint-Sauveur in the city, where we should be able to leave our kayak in safety. "You may book a hotel from here if you like," he offered.

It seemed the best idea, so we booked a room at a hotel near the canal, and then hurried to make sure we reached the marina before it closed.

The canal carried its avenue of plane trees into the heart of the city. But graffiti here marked the walls. We paddled beneath barricaded encampments and swathes of litter where homeless people stared down at us from the towpath under bridges.

Safe at Port Saint-Sauveur, Toulouse.

When the canal widened at the marina, where boats lay parked alongside floating docks, we sought a place to land. There we spotted the *Silver Steel,* a boat we had already met a couple of times before. The English people on board offered to keep an eye on our kayak overnight if we left it nearby. But they urged us to hurry to find the harbormaster before he left for the night. Having found him, we borrowed a key to the marina gate for the morning. Now, with our plans falling into place, we relaxed.

Leaving our kayak safely moored, we carried only a few essentials with us to find our hotel. It felt strange to walk along city streets dressed as we were, to check in at a hotel, to unlock a room with a shower and a bed for the night. But we made the most of it, content to eat in our room instead of hitting a restaurant in town in t-shirts and shorts. We relaxed with a bottle of red wine and stared from the window at the big full moon hanging above the lights of the city.

Paul Riquet statue, Toulouse.

15. Toulouse in Fall

In an unknown secret corner of the sky it floated,
as if in a harbor of the Happy Isles. [18]

Officially the 23rd of September was the first day of fall in Europe. We slipped out of the hotel after coffee and walked alongside the canal to scout ahead. Portaging, if we had to, would be awkward in the city. At the southwest end of Pont Riquet, we found the white marble statue of Riquet between the road carriageways. He stood on a plinth, his back to the canal. His remarkable contribution to this city was honored here.

Having returned to check out of the hotel, we slipped through the marina gates and onto the pontoon to find our kayak safe and still loaded ready to go. When we returned the marina key, the harbormaster told us that there would be a lockkeeper strike today, but only affecting those locks up-canal from here. All boats heading toward the Mediterranean would have to wait, but in our direction, we were free.

He now phoned the locks ahead to say we were coming, but those lockkeepers decided our kayak could not pass through their locks. We would have to portage. He turned back to us, shrugged his shoulders, and apologized. "I am unable to help," he conceded. "Lockkeepers are lockkeepers."

We paddled the mile or so to the first lock, opposite the railway station, and climbed out. With no better way to lift the kayak up the vertical wall onto the stone quay, we unloaded it, and slid the empty kayak over the edge, using the seat pad for protection.

Crossing the fence, and now among the pedestrians, we reloaded the kayak and strapped it onto our new wheels.

Taking the kayak for walk through Toulouse.

Feeling like jailbreakers we set off down the street alongside the high fence and bushes that hid the canal. It felt strange to thread our kayak between passengers getting on and off buses. Trucks and cars rushed past just feet away as we walked our twenty-foot-long pet along the city street. Crossing at traffic lights we rolled past benches where countless cigarette ends littered the ground.

When we could access the canal once more, it lay in a cutting below a high steep bank, presenting a challenging launch. Here was not the most pristine section of the Canal du Midi, but it soon marked the end of it, for the Canal du Midi comes to a three-way junction two miles on from the railway station. It offered us a final opportunity to take a wrong turn.

The wrong way for us would be the Canal de Brienne, opened in 1776, which runs for just short of a mile through Toulouse to join the Garonne River. The connection supplies water from the river to the lateral Canal de Garonne. Water comes from the river just above the *bazacle*, a structure used as an early fording place from the twelfth century onwards, and the site of a later weir.

Five hundred yards upstream from it is the Port-de-la-Daurade, a city dock. When the Canal de Brienne opened, small boats from the canal could avoid having to portage around the weir to access the upper Garonne.

The alternative to entering the Canal de Brienne is the Canal de Garonne, the route we were to take. But how did cargoes reach the Garonne River, on their way downstream to Bordeaux, before completion of the Canal de Garonne?

The Canal du Midi stops abruptly 260 yards from the river. A motorway sweeps in from the north to cross the river right here. Was the canal ever connected by lock to the Garonne? In my research, I have not yet been able to find out. In the early days, did all canal goods traveling through Toulouse offload here to reload onto other craft on the river? Both the Canal de Brienne and the

Canal de Garonne came later. Without the canal de Brienne, were cargoes bound upstream carted to Port-de-la-Daurade above the weir? It seems more likely to me that a lock accessed the river, but if so, why is it no longer there?

The map shows that across the road, behind a row of buildings on the south side of the pool, lie two long canal-like pools, parallel to the one we floated on. They connect with the Canal de Brienne, but with no boat access. What was their purpose, I wondered? Were they holding pools to supply water to the locks downhill? Were they once river docks?

On the wall between where the Canal du Midi and the Canal de Brienne enter from beneath the road bridges, les ponts Jumeaux, is a white marble bas relief. It serves as an epilogue to an elegant canal that carries its avenues of plane trees from near the Mediterranean right into the city. Yet here was no bustle of commerce, or stately canal architecture, simply a turn-around pool. And since the entrance to the Canal de Garonne opens so close to where the Canal du Midi enters, all but the smallest boats must stop and turn around before passing from one to the other.

A high-sided, black, working barge slept here. In front of it, a river tour boat sat idle, its clear vinyl windows secured against intrusion or rain. Smaller boats had moored over at the other side, where a few cars and camper vans parked nearby on the quay.

I looked at the bridges and noted the elegance of the layers of thin bricks, finished in stone. The whitish stone edging of the bridge arches was in alternating blocks: limestone, and a creamy yellow sandstone

Conversation was difficult above the continual roar of traffic. Fast moving vehicles climbed the motorway as it took off to cross the Garonne. Stop-start traffic flowed across the bridges, ponts Jumeaux, and the bridge crossing the entrance to the Canal de Garonne. A road ran along the length of the southern side of the pool. Above the city trees, a somber grey sky set an industrial mood I looked forward to escaping.

"Which way do you think we should go?" asked Kristin, turning to see me, a quirky smile on her face. She remembered the round lock.

"Look, the lady in the bas relief is pointing," I said. "She has her back to the Canal de Brienne. We just came under that bridge, from the Canal du Midi, and she is pointing to the other one, over there. She is our *Garonne Pointing Sign*, GPS."

We began paddling again, into a canal that ran laser-straight for two-and-three-quarters miles (4.5km). The motorway ran alongside for most of the way, while a railway soon joined us from the other side to also follow the canal. Eventually the canal wavered, making a gentle shift toward the left to reveal another long straight run.

I missed the curves in the canal, the plane trees, and the soft color of the stonework of the Canal du Midi bridges and other structures. Here, factories stood beyond the railway, guarded behind chain-link fences. A cycleway ran straight along the other bank. The graffiti, homeless camps under bridges, and litter, made me long for the countryside again. Kristin was grumpy and I could see why.

Yet Toulouse is not a grubby city. It has wonderful architecture and arts, much to commend it. Our mode of travel, budget, and tight schedule were limiting us to the view of Toulouse as seen from the canals.

La ville rose, or *the pink city* as it inadequately translates into English, is a rosy-glow city of reddish brick and white stone. The colors of the brick, and white stone, blend in the eye to appear pink.

The Toulouse bricks are unusual in their dimensions and in their origin. Clay for French bricks, dug and shaped, normally came from the nearest clay pit. It was usual to fire the required bricks in the vicinity of each building project. In that way there is some uniformity of brick color and size within each village. Yet, even when all the clay comes from one place, the final brick color varies according to the duration of firing.

The river basins of the Garonne and the Tarn offer a ready supply of clay for brickmaking, but not in Toulouse. So the city used bricks cast elsewhere in bulk by specialists and then transported into the city.

Bricks from the Tarn and Garonne basins vary from pink through to dark red. The longer the bricks were kiln-fired, the redder the final color. Each town in the region tended to have a consistent brick color, somewhere along the color scale according to its kiln practices. Builders of the finest structures sought bricks of consistent dimensions and color.

These bricks, fired in ovens, or kilns, are *foraines*. The word derives from the French word for an oven, *le four*. Each foraine resembles a Roman brick but is bigger than those usually found in France. Like a Roman brick, it is a cross between a brick as I know it from England, and a tile.

In dimensions, a foraine measures about fourteen and a half inches long, by eight and a half inches wide, by two inches thick. Each weigh about eighteen pounds. (37cm x 22cm x 5.5cm weighing 8 or 9kg).

In addition to using bricks, builders brought stone into the city for the best buildings. With no nearby source, this was expensive. In most cases, stone only edged the brick walls, windows, and doors for adornment. Buildings were rarely all of stone. The white stone came from the Haut Garonne in the Pyrenees.

In the nineteenth century the Virebent brothers, Toulouse architects, patented a method of pressing clay to create decorative façade details. They coated these rough clay moldings in a layer of fine clay. Fired, the pieces mimicked the appearance of the expensive white stone.

They began to prefabricate whole sections of façade to fasten to the front of a building. Buildings, from then onward, could more affordably imitate the expensive, ornately carved, stone window, arches, lintels, and statues. Many buildings in Toulouse used this, architecturally visually consistent, alternative.

Toulouse owes much of its former prosperity to pastel, which is a blue dye extracted from the woad plant, *Isatis tinctoria*. The plant is a member of the brassica family, like cabbage, mustard, and oilseed rape. As such, its yellow flowers may well look familiar even if you have never seen woad before. Its leaves, indicative of the dye, have a blue green tinge. It is necessary to crush the leaves with hot water and soda ash to extract the dye.

The triangle between Albi to the northeast, Carcassonne, and Toulouse, became the most productive woad-growing region. Sales of pastel paid for some of the most sumptuous dwellings in Toulouse.

The fortunes faded. In the eighteenth century, indigo from America, extracted from the indigo plant: *Indigofera tinctoria,* caused the decline of the pastel industry. Then, from 1882, a synthetic blue dye took over the market. But for a while, pastel was a boon to cities like Toulouse.

Woad still grows wild across Europe and has found its way to America too. There, often classified as a class-A noxious weed, eradication is mandatory whenever found.

"Cachou?" Kristin asked, pausing her paddling, and unzipping the pocket of her float vest.

"Bless you." I replied automatically. "Are you suffering from a sneezure?"

Kristin turned, reaching back to pass me a small flat round yellow tin, overprinted in black, at once familiar. "Where did you get this from?" I asked, twisting the top of the tin to line up the holes on the side, and shaking out a tiny black square of licorice."

"Toulouse, of course. Look at the label."

"Cachou, Lajaunie pharmacien, Toulouse France," I read. "I didn't know they were made in Toulouse!" The familiar strong salty licorice flavor hit my mouth. It carried more force than expected from such a small morsel.

Kristin smiled smugly as I passed her back the tin. We resumed paddling, pushing on until we reached the countryside, passing villages and church towers again. At last I felt free of the city.

The Silver Steel passed us, cheering us on. We began to see wildlife again, a muskrat, frogs, a big vole, tussock grasses and kingfishers. We passed mills, and huge barns, while pushing onward and scouting for a suitable place to stop. But as the day faded, we saw nowhere inviting.

At Grisolles, we spotted the Silver Steel moored up for the night. Seeing us approach, they called us over, encouraging us to stop.

"You can camp next to the boat," they offered. "There's a patch of grass by the path. You can use our toilet."

We stopped to look and decided to stay. They suggested we camped on the narrow strip of mown grass that lay between the canal path, used by pedestrians and cyclists, and the road. Across the road, flower beds and small trees decorated the community center gardens.

Such a place to camp was hardly private, yet we felt companionship beside the boat. We hurriedly arranged the tent with the kayak beside it, now lit by streetlamps.

Even after dark I felt we were very much in the public eye. The community center, just a few yards away, was busy with people coming and going until late. Individuals lingered on the canal path, with unleashed dogs which always investigated both kayak and tent. Cyclists, cars, and trains rushed by.

16. Thunder

Yet come, dark thunderstorms,
And brood your heavy hours;
For when you rain me words,
My thoughts are dancing flowers
And joyful singing birds. [19]

A bright flash preceded the rumble of thunder in the distance. Gradually the flashes became brighter, and the crashes followed sooner. The storm was getting closer. I slipped out to tension the guy-lines around the tent and ducked inside again just in time. The rattle of the deluge hit, the heavy drops shaking the tent and drowning any other sounds from outside. Brilliant flashes of lightning flared, momentarily bringing daylight crispness. The claps of thunder felt visceral.

Everything was still wet after the storm when at first light we prepared espresso, before setting off to explore the village. There, the magnificent cast iron framework and decorative brickwork of a nineteenth century covered marketplace stood empty. The church, its walls alternating between fine horizontal bands of brick and white stone, overall appeared pale pink. It reminded me of a delicate gâteau. It pointed a knobby spire to the sky.

Standing before a terraced building, I marveled at the perfect patina; disintegration manipulated into an art form. Here, the stucco façade was crumbling away exposing the brickwork beneath. For economy, the underlayer consisted of alternate layers of single foraines held apart by small brick spacers. Rough cement infilled the voids in the alternate layers, except around the windows where the brickwork was complete. Closed shutters of darkened bare wood hung on rusted stable hinges. The effect was pleasing in its sense of fulfilment, like an old man comfortable in a darned sweater, relaxing back into the embrace of a threadbare armchair.

If the building were under restoration, I could see no sign of haste. Next door, a small hardware store showed how the original building might have looked. Render neatly covered the wall to the edge of an exposed brickwork border around each window.

Another building had alternate layers of red brick, and rounded river stones. An ironwork cross stood tall supporting a weathercock on top, a pigeon resting on its tail.

But it was the patina that made the deepest impression upon me. It encapsulated time. It embodied the sadness of men lost to war, those absent children who might have restored so much. We can embrace the rapid changes that bring in the new, but there is much to appreciate in the changes that time brings gradually, the inexorable disintegration toward entropy.

The museum, closed, was in an old building. Brick walls around the ground floor held up a timber frame floor which jutted out above. The spaces between the timbers were infilled artistically using bricks.

Some shops were open, so we bought enough for breakfast on our way back to the canal, where we saw no movement on the Silver Steel. Hearing bursts of loud music from the community center, we walked over there to use their facilities instead.

The Silver Steel still sat silent as slumber when we slipped away along the canal, just in time before the rain began again. Yet the boat caught up nine miles later at the next lock where, in the absence of a lockkeeper, they helped us through. We bid them farewell there, for they moored before the next set of locks, just a few yards farther on, where they prepared to explore on land.

The canal at Montech drops through a series of five locks in one-and-a-half miles which can take an hour for a boat to pass through. A ramp opened beside the locks in 1974 to allow larger vessels to pass quicker. Boats up to 130 feet long (40 meters) can use the ramp, while smaller boats use the locks.

The Montech locomotives with gate raised.

Two diesel railway locomotives work in harness, yoked together by a metal framework above. Like the later engine at the Béziers' Fonserannes water slope, they run along the walls of the ramp on tyres, not rails. A hydraulic ram lifts a gate to allow a boat to enter at the bottom of the slope. The gate drops into place behind. A cushioned brace, lowered between the two locomotives between the gate and the boat, pushes the boat up the ramp.

The gate has seals on the sides and underneath to capture a wedge of water which the locomotives push all the way to the top of the rise, the boat still floating.

Once the boat reaches the top, the chamber there equalizes to the water level in the canal, the gates open, and the boat can leave. Then everything is ready for a boat to enter at the top for descent.

"I think we should portage the whole section in one," I suggested. "Otherwise as soon as we've launched for each bit, it'll be time to get out again."

Kristin agreed, "It'll make a pleasant change to walk!" So we strapped the kayak to the wheels and strolled downhill. At the bottom we left the kayak and went to see the two massive blue and white locomotives in their frame. The huge gate was open, raised. The perspective made the long concrete slope appear to narrow toward the lock gates at the top. These engines can push 53,000 cubic feet (1,500 cubic meters) of water up the hill at 2.8 mph. (4.5km per hour). The ramp is much quicker than negotiating the flight of locks, a boat can pass from bottom to top in just six minutes.

"Those machines look so powerful! Actually, the whole structure seems unreal!" In a way it reminded me of the grape-harvesting machines we saw out in the fields, each straddling a row of vines with the wheels in the corridors either side.

The Montech water slide from below.

Seven miles and three locks farther on we reached the ancient city of Castelsarrasin, where we saw an opportunity to shop. People chatted on deck on the boats moored at a pontoon beside a park, so we felt safe leaving the kayak and walking away together. As a treat we bought pain au chocolat, along with our usual bread, cheese, and wine. We added fruit, a cucumber and duck pâté. But, stepping outside the store we found ourselves in a downpour.

"Let's shelter," Kristin wisely suggested. "I think it's just a shower. We might be able to avoid getting soaked."

We stood in the doorway until the shower passed and then made our way gingerly back, our plastic clogs treacherous on the slick wet surfaces.

A fountain sprayed in the park, where a lawn of immaculately manicured grass spread from the canal. Ducks busied themselves everywhere, keeping the grass clipped, and fertilized, all around big pots overflowing with flowers. We had found the ideal place to linger over lunch, enjoying duck liver pâté and cucumber with our baguette while watching the ducks.

Near the end of the day we saw a rosy glow from the canal ahead. As we drew closer, we could see the glow was from the sun hitting reddish walls that bordered the canal into the distance. We were approaching the aqueduct that crosses the River Tarn. When we reached it, we stopped and got out to look over the side.

It is a beautiful seven-arched structure of warm, pink, Toulouse brick, edged in white Quercy stone, which stretches for some three-hundred-and-fifty yards. From the sunlit side, the rich color radiated a warm glow. We looked downstream to the next bend in the river, beyond which, in three and a half miles from here, the Tarn would flow into the Garonne.

Jumping back into the kayak we crossed the canal and landed again to see upstream. The low-angle sunlight shone from under the arches, setting the green water aglow. Two hundred yards upstream the railway, having doggedly followed the canal since Toulouse, crossed the river over a white-painted girder bridge.

Hearing a boat engine I turned. A green-hulled pénichette, one of the small-sized French style canal barges, was approaching along the canal from the Toulouse direction. We watched it pass. It began to follow the ribbon of water across the aqueduct.

"Wow! Look how it's weaving!" I exclaimed as it almost hit the stonework but veered sharply away. "It must be windy there!"

We both stood and watched it zigzag as each gust caught its superstructure and blew it sideways. When it reached the far end of the aqueduct, looking much diminished in size, it vanished between the trees.

Beyond the aqueduct the canal runs above dense lines of trees and bushes: fields of fruit. A silvery gossamer of netting hung loosely across the plants to prevent damage to the fruit in heavy rain and hailstorms. Moissac, the town we were approaching, is known for its cultivation of Chasselas table grapes.

Thunder

We portaged two deep locks and, having taken out at a third at the edge of town, found ourselves at a canal junction. A cut of 150 yards, mostly taken up by a double lock, led down to the River Tarn.

I remembered how our cycle map, a basic map of the whole canal at a small scale, had shown a campground before Moissac. It seemed sensible to book a site there for the night. We would be perfectly situated to visit the town in the morning, but where was my map, and where was the campground? We walked the path to a canal junction and followed the branch to the River Tarn.

"I can't see any campground," I complained, frustrated by how well it hid. "You would expect to find a signpost at least."

Some six hundred yards downstream, across the Tarn, was an elegant bridge: Pont Napoléon. This road bridge, completed in 1829, was in a similar style to the brick and stone arched aqueduct we crossed earlier. The low sun reflected up from the water, almost silhouetting the bridge, although by squinting we could see the detail.

Greeting a woman out walking her dog, we asked about the campground. "It is over on the other side," she pointed across the river, "not near here." She looked at our puzzled faces. "You have a car?"

"No, we are kayaking along the canal." She looked us up and down thoughtfully.

"You can camp near my house by the canal if you like," she offered. "I live up that way, two locks up the canal."

We joined her, walking back beside the canal, towing our kayak at the pace of her little dog until, just before the gates of the second lock, she veered off away from the canal. She led us along a little path beneath trees toward where her house stood cozily in a hollow below, surrounded by a lovely, landscaped garden. "I live down there, but perhaps you can camp up here. Is this, okay? You can come down to use my toilet. I will leave the door open for you in the night. Come in, I'll show you."

Before we left her house to pitch our tent, she handed us a bag of her home-grown tomatoes and wished us a good sleep.

We prepared the tent beneath the trees, stumbling over big green frogs in the dark. The sound of water rushing over or through the closed lock gates murmured a lullaby.

Aqueduct over the river Tarn.

17. Moissac

Ne that a monk, whan he is cloisterlees,
Is lykned til a fish that is waterlees;[20]

The pleasing sound of tumbling water greeted my ears. The water continued to run from the adjacent lock gates. The air smelled fresh and sweet beneath the trees as we rolled up our tent. Our next task of the day was to portage to below the next lock, six hundred yards away, and to reach the water over a wooden fence and down a precipitous grassy slope. Had we not belayed the stern to the fence as we maneuvered down, we might have ended up in the canal instead of on it.

We had not far to paddle to a small marina, just across the canal, which offered a place for us to land again. The harbormaster, a lanky Englishman in red shorts, greeted us amiably, informing us that, although he had closed the office, he would open the showers for us later. If we could find him. He pointed the way to the shops.

Kristin was excited. "The Moissac church and cloisters are famous!" she said. "I have a book about them at home. The stone carvings are exceptional. I did not realize we would be here. I'd really like to see them."

We walked across town, much of the way along a narrow, cobbled street. We found the church just a half mile away, at the other side of the town: an imposing building of brick and white stone in Romanesque style. We stood before the south entrance in wonder at the tympanum. Carved from a creamy yellow stone, it portrays the apocalypse. This was not a feature of the original abbey, which had fallen into disrepair by the early eleventh century. The abbey, an important stop on a pilgrimage route, needed restoration when a twelfth century renaissance ushered in the High Middle Ages. This doorway and tympanum dates from between 1115-1135.

When standing close enough to the entrance to appreciate the expressions on the carved faces, I could not grasp the proportions of the massive building. Walking away for a longer view, I sized it up. It was huge. No little breeze could blow away the history of this town from beneath such a hefty paperweight.

Entering the nave, everything glowed golden yellow, the walls appearing like a skin of gilded scales. First climbing the spiral staircase to a balcony to view the nave from a different angle, we next made our way to the cloister. Here was a place of serenity, the arches of the cloisters supported by alternating single and double slender columns surrounding a quadrangle of grass. A stately tree, I thought to be a cedar of Lebanon, stood to one side.

At first all I was aware of was the wonderful sense of calm, the pleasing overall impression of all those repeated archways. I felt I could easily sit down and relax here for a year or two.

"If you look at the capitals, you'll see how each carving tells a different story," Kristin pointed out, calling attention to the details above the columns of the cloister. "There are some stories carved on a few of the columns too, but not so many." As I strolled slowly along examining each, I began to see what she meant.

Cloisters at Moissac Abbey.

Carved Capitals at Moissac Abbey.

The waters of history often muddy the origin of a building such as this. Some say that the Frankish King Clovis founded a monastery here in 506AD in memory of his victory over the Visigoths: That he wanted one thousand monks to stay in memory of the thousand troops he lost in the battle. Others say St Didier, the bishop of Cahors, founded the monastery in the mid-seventh century.

If the cloister felt peaceful today, there could be no more guarantee of tranquility here tomorrow than there was in its past.

Since the founding of the monastery, hostile groups from all directions have arrived to loot it. Norman pirates raided from the north, Arabs from the Iberian Peninsula to the south, and Hungarians from the east.

Despite those raids, successive Benedictine monks, the black monks, stayed here for an almost continuous thousand years. Ironically, it was Augustinian monks who finally forced them out. The monastery continued to be active under the new order until the French Revolution stopped all monastic life. Now the buildings are open to all to visit, but for how long? Who knows what will become of the buildings in the next few hundred years?

Moissac is an important stop on one of the pilgrimage routes to Santiago de Compostela in Spain, popular in the Middle Ages, and many of the tourists we saw bore the scallop shell symbol associated with that trail.

With regret, we left the serenity of the cloisters to make our way out into the bustling world of the Moissac market.

The public market was in full swing, with crowds hustling. Shoppers leaned and reached, selecting from the colorful local produce stacked high on the stalls. Stall keepers called greetings, calculated, and wrapped, held out a palm for cash and rummaged for change. Crates of fungi piled high on one table. Boleti, sorted by size, surrounded the crates. The biggest ones, massive specimens of boletus edulis (cèpe de Bordeaux), lay artfully spread on a bed of bracken beside a crate of orange chanterelles. The wonderful musty, slightly apricot, aroma reminded me that despite the festive summer atmosphere, autumn was upon us.

Coins tumbled into metal cash boxes, amid the muffled swish of shopping bags and baskets. Couples quietly conferred about decisions, while sellers called out for attention.

Here were braids of plump garlic, bunches of purple-and-white radishes, nut-brown chicken eggs piled high in a basket, melons and squashes, yellow green grapes, and boxes of filberts. The air smelled strongly of fruit and vegetable. Sometimes I caught a more pungent whiff of a market smell, like sour garlic or onion on a breath.

We eased our way past chickens, strung by their necks, and rabbits, soon finding what we needed. Then we slipped into the adjacent wine market where we waved repeatedly to catch the attention of the vintner. The tall paunchy man, wearing a burgundy apron over a navy sweatshirt, stood pouting a fat-lipped frown between a heavy moustache and triple chins while staring blankly at something far away or in another day.

Retracing our way through the narrow streets to the dock, we were soon afloat, our way confined deep inside a brick-walled cut through town. The sides of this cutting were so deep that the canal-side roads did not need to rise to cross at the bridges.

Some of the people navigating the canal were clearly novice boaters, but not all. Here we followed a group as they began their holiday aboard a rental boat. A big Swiss flag emblazoned on the apron of one of the women gave a clue to her nationality. This team looked organized; each person focused on their own task.

"Look how she's swabbing the decks while the other woman is washing the windows," Kristin observed. "They've even brought potted geraniums to make the boat look nice, and they're getting everything clean and tidy from the start!"

Our view opened beyond Moissac, yet like a bundle of cables, the canal, the roads either side, and the railway, all followed the river. Trees lined the grassy banks. We caught up with the Swiss group again and joined them through the first lock, watching how they worked the mechanism themselves in the absence of a lockkeeper. They began the process at a pole dangling over the river on a wire.

When we arrived alone at the next lock, the Swiss group were long gone, so we tried to go through it by ourselves. The pole hung well out of reach, at a reasonable elevation for someone on a canal boat. If all it needed was a gentle tug, then maybe we could achieve that by swinging the pole. Reaching a paddle in the air, we managed to bat it a few times, and to our delight the lock began to fill. Once the gates opened, the light changed from red to green and we were on our way in.

"What are we supposed to do now?" I asked.

"I expect the controls are over there," Kristin pointed to a roofed structure above a notice board. "I saw something similar at the last lock, with one of the Swiss people standing by it."

Kristin hopped out of the kayak and found the button to start the mechanism, but nothing happened when she pressed it. She waited and tried again to no avail.

"I'll look to see if there is a sensor somewhere that can detect when a boat enters," I suggested, spinning the kayak around to see if I could spot anything. Sure enough I found one, but the kayak was too low to activate it.

"Try holding your paddle down. It probably needs to be blocked for more than a few seconds to imitate a boat, and it's awkward to do from down here. I keep floating away when I hold my paddle up."

Kristin reached down to cover the sensor with her paddle blade. Having blocked it for about twelve seconds she returned to press the button, and sure enough, the gates swung into action.

I quickly maneuvered to the side to let Kristin hop into her seat. As soon as the gates closed, the water level began to fall, exposing the slimy wall. Level after level of stonework appeared before the water steadied. The far gates began to swing open, the lights changed from red to green, and we were on our way cheering our good fortune. We could manage locks by ourselves! Or so we thought.

The canal hugs the river Garonne as far as the village of Malause, where the river divides into two and follows its northern section. The wider river route loops south before returning north to rejoin the straighter channel.

We soon found that our lock opening success had been a fluke. We could not open any other. To compound my disappointment, at each portage, my back hurt. I must have twisted it, lifting the kayak high enough to put the trolley underneath, or take it away. Now I found even pulling the kayak on land painful.

Valence d'Agen, has an early nineteenth century oval public washhouse that we were interested to see. *Lavoir Saint-Bernard* stands two hundred yards walk from a bridge over the canal. It is a spring-fed, circular, pool open to the sky, ringed by an outward-sloping pantiled roof. This roof dates from 1924, built to shelter the washers. The pool's cobbled surround is at a level lower than the sidewalk, enclosed by a supporting wall of Toulouse brick. A drinking trough for horses was once available here too.

Three public washhouses serve Valence d'Agen. All lie along the contour of the hill where the freshwater springs rise. The Saint-Bernard washhouse is the first from upstream, but the other two are just a short walk from the quay by the next bridge, Le Lavoir Del Théron is round, while the third in the line, Le Lavoir du Pé de Gleyze is rectangular.

Public washhouse at Valence d'Agen.

These washhouses offer clean fresh water. But not all washhouses along the way were spring fed. Some were alongside the canal and used canal water. The concrete counters of these roofed shelters are just above water level. They would reach to between waist and chest-height of someone stood inside. Were these for local people, or for those traveling along the canal? Some looked like open-fronted concrete bunkers, while others had brick walls and dark timber supports at the front. All had clay-tiled roofs.

Standing inside afforded a unique perspective of the canal, from such a low angle. Dragonflies patrolled, darting down to snatch prey, and blue damselflies alighted at the water's edge. With my elbows on the cement shelf, my head resting in my hands, I drifted into contemplation.

Evening adds urgency to the quest for a camp spot, when necessity narrows the field. Our choice tonight felt safe, our tent sandwiched between the canal and the railway, but houses stood opposite.

"I think we'll be okay here. It will soon be dark, and we will leave early, so I don't think we'll offend anybody."

We had not seen anyone else camping beside the canal, nor met anyone traveling as we did, in a human-powered craft. But in the cool of the early morning we heard the rhythmic creak and splash of rowers. We watched them speed through the mist that clung to the water. When we set off soon after, the air felt crispy cool, and the water warm to our fingers. Gradually the sun gathered in the trees.

Looking into washhouse.

Washhouse beside canal.

18. Agen

If the ocean were whisky,
And I was a duck,
I'd dive to the bottom
And never come up[21]

Philippe Wielgus, a Belgian man who lived in north Agen, greeted us as we passed his boat in the canal basin at Agen. We had skirted a row of rental boats, moored stern to quay between narrow pontoons. We were looking for a place to land, to find a shower and to recharge our camera batteries. Philippe, spending a week on his boat, *Lotus Betula*, with his two sons, helped orient us.

He was a man who looked as if he would know what was going on around here. Moments later, a group of Australians approached him seeking tourist information. He steered them on their way too.

While landed, Kristin ran into town to shop. "Look," she showed me when she got back. "I found these at the open market. They are local. Try one." From the paper bag I lifted a fat wrinkled prune. It tasted sweet and juicy.

Agen is known for its prunes, although they grow in the surrounding region, not right here. The Romans first planted the Maurine, a small blue plum, which dries to a very dark prune. Much later, in the twelfth century, Benedictine monks brought back the Damas plum from Syria after the third crusade. They grafted it onto the earlier rootstocks for a plum that dried into the larger Prune d'Ente, the *grafted prune*.

Since prunes keep well, it was easy to ship them from the Port of Agen down the Garonne to Bordeaux, and from there, around the world. They arrived at Bordeaux from Agen, so when exported, they were known as *Agen prunes*.

If this area became known for its prunes, it is also known for Armagnac, a type of brandy less well known than Cognac. This liquor, distilled from wine in the area just west of Agen, has the longest unbroken history of production of any liquor in the world.

Small local businesses still produce Armagnac, using column stills. In the past, distillers carried their stills by cart from farm to farm. They enabled local people to produce their own Armagnac, from their own wine, without having to buy the equipment, or learn all the tricks of the trade.

Although the usual way to enjoy Armagnac, like Cognac, is to sip it from a glass, local restaurants serve a special dessert of Agen prunes soaked in Armagnac. But Armagnac is also an integral part of a traditional French gourmet dish, only recently banned. Hunters catch the ortolan bunting alive, in nets, while the small bird is on migration. When boxed and kept in the dark for three or four weeks, these birds gorge themselves on millet, fattening up.

Once the birds are plump, the chef drowns them in Armagnac and leaves them in it to marinate. Roasted for eight minutes, plucked, and served whole, each bunting is one mouthful.

Since a serving consists of a single bird, and chefs consider it gluttony to order two, some stuff the little body with foie gras and a little piece of truffle to make the most of the decadent morsel.

The étiquette for dining is to hold the bird by its head and to eat the body whole, spitting out any bones too hard to chew. It is customary to hide behind, or under, a napkin while eating. A sensible custom, not only so you can deal with bones discreetly, but also to hide your face from recognition, since the dish is illegal.

The European government banned hunting of the bird in 1979, but it took another twenty years before France imposed the ban. That ban has been slow to take effect, with lobbying to persuade the French government to make it legal again.

Using brandy as a marinade has a history. Apart from imparting flavor, brandy is a preservative. Following the Battle of Trafalgar off southwest Spain in 1805, a ship carried the body of Lord Horatio Nelson back to England, in a barrel of brandy, before burial. I assume the oak barrel contributed tannins to the brandy: Lord Nelson added body.

We would forego eating buntings in Armagnac, but since Kristin's surname is Nelson, it seemed proper for me to ask if she would like the same treatment as her namesake. She said that rather than climbing into a tub of brandy she would apply Armagnac just a little at a time: internally, sip by sip.

Lord Nelson, unlike the little birds, was already dead before immersion in alcohol. However it is rumored that King Edward IV of England gave his twenty-eight-year-old brother, the Duke of Clarence, the bunting treatment. The story tells how the King had the duke imprisoned, in the Tower of London, before, in 1478, ordering him executed by drowning in a butt of Malmsey, fortified wine from Madeira.

Philippe offered us coffee, so we joined him, sitting beside his boat, talking. Our journey intrigued him, and he wanted our adventure to inspire his sons.

The canal narrows a mile from the Agen canal basin. Here is the start of the 1849 aqueduct that carries the canal six hundred yards across the valley, over the river Garonne. Since the canal is too narrow for boats to pass here, boats must wait their turn from each direction. We followed a pénichette, its bicycles strapped to the deck, chasing it as far as the locks beyond the aqueduct to go through them with it.

The Frenchman at the bow looped his mooring line deftly around the bollard and secured it. The woman at the stern threw her line but missed. With the bow captured, the stern swung like a door closing across the lock. The man strode calmly to the stern to take and recoil the line. He flicked it around the bollard for her, hauling the boat straight once more.

Having watched the scenario play out once, we prudently held back at the following locks. I was glad, since the woman invariably missed. Had we followed too closely the stern would have sideswiped us.

We were paddling ahead of a South African party. They looked serious, being cautious at the start of their first day afloat.

The French boat soon pulled away and the South African boat passed us slowly and carefully. Then from behind came a Canadian group from Vancouver, British Columbia. They were in a hurry, churning past us to come up short behind the South African boat.

Weaving from side to side to try to see ahead, they gunned forward, squeezing alongside. When they realized they would never make the next bend, they fell back.

They tried several times until, on a straighter section, they opened the throttle and went for it. However, these canal boats cannot get up much speed, especially in the shallow confines. Evidently pushing as fast as possible, their speed was still not much greater than the other boat. With little room to spare, they reached the bow wave of the slower boat. Thrown off course by the wave, they zigzagged, ploughing through overhanging foliage and bringing down all kinds of greenery.

We laughed. Leaves and debris adorned the Canadians' boat and littered the canal. Undeterred, the Canadians forged onward, disentangling branches from their guardrails. For all their trouble, they were not much faster than the South Africans, who caught them up at the next lock.

We reached Buzet-sur-Baize near the end of the day to find quite a lively evening scene. The little canal port here is on a strip of land between the canal and the Baize River, with a lock offering river access. The Baize joins the Garonne a little more than two miles away.

The Canadian tree-trimmers had stopped here for the night and were partying outside the restaurant. Camper vans and boats clustered around. We hopped out onto a narrow wooden walkway and tethered the kayak. We needed drinking water, but since Buzet has its own wine appellation, it seemed appropriate to also buy a bottle of local red wine. Red accounts for most of the local production.

Drifting afloat again, we admired a wooden barge moored opposite, and complimented the Dutch couple on board. They told us they were exploring all around Europe. This was their third year so far; traveling in summer and finding somewhere comfortable to moor up each winter until spring. They had been in Holland, Belgium, and now France. They planned to start returning slowly north again next year.

"Come join us on board for a glass of wine," they invited. Tempted, we regretfully declined. The sun had already set, and we had found no place to camp yet.

Woodland with undergrowth guarded the next section, discouraging us from landing. Deer watched from the shore, and we heard the gunshots of hunters, which made the prospect of camping in the dark woodland uninviting.

I was relieved to reach the canal pool and marina at Damazan, to find a quiet spot across the river from most of the moored boats. Having cut a few brambles by flashlight to prepare a tent spot, we settled in for dinner in the tent uncorking the bottle of Buzet wine.

"Drinking Buzet near Buzet," said Kristin thoughtfully, as she read the wine label. "Cheers!"

Owls hooted, and I could not resist returning their calls. Soon one settled quite close.

Kristin brews espresso, Damazan.

19. Damazan

Many sheltered within
When I dreamed myself a castle[22]

Waking before sunrise, we watched the mist rising like steam from the canal in the chill of morning. Beams of sunlight eventually began sloping through the trees, setting the foliage aglow, and dappling through here and there to reach the leaf-carpeted ground. I pored over the canal book, jotted notes in my journal and sipped espresso.

Damazan is an English bastide. Its name, when founded in 1259 by Alfonse, the Count of Toulouse and of Poitiers, was Castrum Comitale. That name hints of fortification. Alfonse built many of the bastides around here, following the devastation of the Albigensian war. Damazan was in the shape of a double cross, aligned north-south, east-west. A market square stood at the center, with the church adjacent.

Nowadays there is only one remaining defensive tower, at the southeast corner, and some fragments of wall, but it was the half-timbered wattle and daub houses, and the sheltered arcades surrounding the town hall, which fascinated me. We sat in the market square beneath the town hall, looking out at the old houses. On the walls of some, thin bricks filled the spaces in the frame between the timbers. Seemingly laid at whatever angle appeared most convenient for each space, the overall effect was higgledy-piggledy.

Market square, Damazan.

The bakery, a single room only large enough for four or five people to stand, displayed a wonderful hedgehog loaf, and fish-tailed baguettes. We bought pastries and managed to reach our kayak before we ate them, stuffing the baguettes into the paddle bag on the front deck for later.

Running into the Canadians we followed yesterday, we learned from them the reason why we were unable to open the locks. The trick is to twist the dangling pole ninety degrees, one-quarter turn, not to pull it.

We joined them to descend several locks until they turned around to go back. Then, stopping at the next lock, we circled underneath the dangling pole looking up at it. "Do you think you could reach it if you stood up?" I asked.

Damazan

"I don't know. I will try it, but not if you keep jiggling like that. I do not want to fall in here. Can you keep the kayak steady?"

It was trickier than I had imagined, to both steady the kayak, and stop it from drifting from under the pole, in the current and wind. The kayak is responsive and will shift from edge to edge with just the lowering of a hip. I suppressed my urge to hold it in balance, freeing Kristin to control with her feet instead.

When she stood up, Kristin needed a full-arm-stretch to reach the pole. Maneuvering, I tried to be as gentle as possible. Every paddle stroke threatened to unbalance her. She grasped the pole, gave it a twist, and crouched quickly back down. She had done it! The lock stirred into action.

We had anticipated the whole procedure, from twisting the pole. Now we waited for the gates to open, and for the lights to change from red to green, so we could enter the lock.

Once safely inside, Kristin would take her paddle to block the sensor, simulating a boat entering, while I remained in the kayak. Having pressed the button to activate the lock, Kristin would have time to rejoin me in the kayak before the gates closed with a final clunk.

We had to be wary when the water level dropped in the locks, for sometimes water spouted from holes between the stone blocks, emptying every hidden void. The penalty for inattention was a dirty-water shower.

The gates opened automatically when we reached the lower level, and when the lights changed to green, we could exit. It was so much easier than a portage.

Ten miles on from Damazan, after a stretch of canal that ran alongside the river Garonne, we reached a port. The quay stood on the right, while on the bluff above, to our left, we could see brick fortifications edging the hilltop. These were the walls, and low round towers, of the village Le Mas d'Agenais. From the Middle Ages, entry was via five defended gates.

Le Mas d'Agenais sits along a limestone terrace above the canal, which is above the river. As one of the oldest, and for a long time most important, villages in the region, it originally stood to the west of its current center.

Originally named Ussubium, when occupied by the Romans from the first to third centuries, it took the new name: Pompeiacum, when it moved to its present location. It changed its name again, to Le Mas d'Agenais, sometime in the eleventh century.

A Roman stele found here bears a Latin inscription referring to the protecting goddess of Ussubium. It is currently on display in the Romanesque church, itself founded in the eleventh century.

One of the more interesting archaeological finds from the early occupation is a Greek-style, white, stone statue of Venus of Mas, from the first century BC. Found here in 1876, it is on display in the museum at Agen.

Le Mas d'Agenais was a ferry point on the river until the building of the suspension bridge, with its yellow stone towers, in 1840. It is interesting to realize how much of a dividing line a river, as soon as it widens, can make across the landscape. A deep river requires a ferry or a bridge to cross, and the wider the river, the more costly the bridge. From here, the next bridging point of the river is at Marmande, nine meandering river miles downstream.

The river has carved a two-and-a-half miles wide corridor across the landscape here, bordered either side by a scarp to higher ground. The canal contours the straightish edge of the higher land to the southwestern side, occasionally passing villages, while towns line the edge of the higher ground at the far side of the river corridor. The Garonne meanwhile winds back and forth across the lower flood plain.

From the kayak, the trunks of the plane trees, which lined both sides, visually overlapped, confining our view ahead. The dappled grey trunks gently curved like ribs in some long skeleton. As we progressed inside the long bony cage, greenery, which met above from both sides, hid the sky. Below, the water, although flat, appeared to drop deeply as it mirrored the archway of trees. Overall, it reminded me of looking into a kaleidoscope, my eyes inexorably swallowed by the distant point at the center.

But the canal bank to our right side was often the highest point of land. Seen between the plane trees was a view, across the flat-bottomed valley, to more distant hillsides. Sometimes we passed close by a farm, or an old church, a moored barge, fields of maize, or rows of plantation trees.

The road from Marmande crosses the canal at Pont du Sable. A large and active rowing club bustled on the left side opposite the canal port, people carrying lightweight rowing shells from the boathouse and balancing them on trestles. There was a neat stack of kayaks ready outside. Arm-powered vessels were a change from the motorized transport we mostly saw.

Richard the Lionheart founded a bastide at Marmande, on the far side of the river, in about 1195, at the site of an earlier settlement. But not long afterwards, in 1219, the Albigensian Crusade took the town and massacred its inhabitants. Affected by many conflicts brought from elsewhere since then, Marmande is now best known for its heirloom beefsteak tomatoes. These tomatoes, released around 1897, have become a European favorite, and are readily available and popular in USA too.

We cruised on, covering miles, and negotiating locks. Kingfishers sparked into low flight, and herons solemnly watched us pass. For a moment we found ourselves beside a school of children, all smartly dressed in white trousers and dark jackets. The fleeting glimpse brought back memories of schoolboy discipline and study.

Where the river swung back across its valley to brush close to the canal again, we reached another village, Meilhan-sur-

Garonne, and took the opportunity to snack at a canal basin beside a campground. Then we pressed on, leaving the river again, the canal once more sheltered beneath trees.

As it grew later, I watched for the right place to stop for the night, but nowhere tempted me. Here and there, permanently parked boats floated beneath the overhanging tree branches. Fallen leaves, rotting, nourished the mosses which offered a generous foothold for weeds and saplings to sprout around the decks. Fields of maize stood beside the canal, and a harvester worked late, its lights already beaming while brightness lingered in the sky.

Pushing faster, I began to grow anxious. We must pick somewhere to stop. In theory, any place would do. But choosing the right place to spend the night can be subtly complex. Over the years I have prided myself on mostly picking a good spot.

In one way, deciding where to camp is like finding a place to sit on a log. On a log, ants may discourage me from sitting at one end, while another part of the log might slope too steeply for comfort. I would avoid a knobbly knot, or a damp patch. Usually there is a sweet spot, offering the most comfortable seat. When you watch a group settle for lunch on a log, the good spots go first. Latecomers perch uncomfortably.

There are other choices to make, such as choosing which way to face. In a café, I favor a place with my back to a wall where I can see the whole room, including the door, without turning around. I avoid the center of the room and am less comfortable with my back to the door. I do not like to be in the path of everyone who enters, but if I must, I prefer to face the entrance.

Seeking a camp spot beside the canal, I look for somewhere with no bank traffic, road, or cycleway, at the inside of a bend rather than outside. Trees, a hedge, or a bank, can create a comforting virtual wall, sheltering from sight any houses or thoroughfares.

Easy place to camp beside the canal.

Overriding everything else is how a place *feels*. Many places we passed conveyed indifference. Any such place might have been okay at a pinch, despite my rejecting them in the search for somewhere better.

Just occasionally something draws me magnetically to a particular place. I at once sense it will be right, and it invariably is.

When I stop to analyze why, I can easily justify, pointing out myriad contributary reasons. It is easy to attribute that intuition to many years of experience, when evaluating what is good about a choice. But is there more to it? When it comes to places that just feel bad, I am often at a loss to explain why.

Why would any place, otherwise apparently great for camping, give the impression it is just waiting for a dead body? Or hint that it is already hiding a murder victim? Why, when strolling through woodland carefree, calm and at peace with the world, might I suddenly pass a spot where the hairs on my neck prickle with a sense of dread? Such places I reject out of hand for no rational reason.

Do we have an innate sense of safe and unsafe? Do we unconsciously smell, see, or hear something that triggers such an alert? In a world where most places seem neutral, why do I perceive some to be *wrong*? How do they so strongly repel?

So, as we paddled along, I scanned the banks for that equivalent of the corner of a room away from the highway, a place neither indifferent nor scary. A cozy place that *felt right*. I did not find one.

It was dark when we reached the next lock. Construction work was clearly under way on the buildings beside the lockkeepers cottage, although paused for the night. Deterred by all the materials and tools spread in front, we landed opposite. But there we found the portage less straightforward than expected.

An overflow channel looped away from the canal, dropping, and eventually rejoining it at the lower level. It diverted and extended the cycleway: our portage route. This cycleway curved uphill from the canal to a junction, continuing to curve gently as it dropped to reach the canal two hundred yards farther along. At its high point, a path from a bridge by the lock crossed the cycle path.

Right at a corner of the crossroad, against a hedgerow of brambles, and bushes, was a small triangle of rough grass behind a signpost. The sign pointed: *Castets 13*. Castets is where the canal would end, where we must join the river.

Here at l'Auriole, the river has meandered close to the canal once again. Beyond our comforting hedge the slope dropped through trees. I could sense the presence of the river, in the temperature and humidity of the air, and from the quiet background sounds.

Damazan

Under the moon and star-lit sky, the calls of owls resounded from the trees. I could hear the tumble of water through the overflow channel between us and the canal. We chose our spot for the night beneath the signpost beside the cycleway. If indifferent, there was nothing more promising available right now.

In the morning Kristin crept out, leaving me barely awake. I soon heard her firing the stove and making coffee. Outside, dew-heavy spider webs drooped from the signpost. More glistened in the long grass and between the brambles in the hedgerow.

"Come on down to see the river," Kristin encouraged brightly. The steep path wound downhill, just fifty yards, past walnut, and apple trees. A rabbit track led down the final drop to a river beach. Mist smothered the water. The sun sent searchlight beams through it from between the trees, illuminating the barely visible gravel banks, fallen trees, and tangled flotsam. Kingfishers flashed past above the riffles on the low river.

"It's really nice down here," I agreed, in no hurry to leave. "Thanks for persuading me to come!"

But by the time we climbed the hill again, the builders had begun work across the canal. Dog-walkers paused at the tent as their dogs sniffed around, and cyclists whirred by. Our camp spot, although good enough for the night, felt out of place this morning. We must move on. Castets-en-Dorthe was just eight miles away and I was eager to reach the river. The end of the canal would mark a big milestone on our journey.

We can finally operate the locks ourselves.

The countryside grew hilly to our left where vines, and maize, added texture and pattern to the patchwork. To our right, the land was flatter across the flood plain of the river. Kristin standing, each lock opened easily at her twist of the dangling baton. Soon enough the canal grew wider for its final mile, grander and tidier. At about fifty yards wide, even barges could turn around here if they chose not to join the river.

At last we reached the long drop of the final lock of the Garonne canal into the river. We saw a red light with no controls. Our final lock descent required a lockkeeper. Beside stood a tall building, the lockkeepers office. Steep staircases curved up both sides and a gauge mounted against the wall between them showed the highest flood levels for different years. Some floods had risen phenomenally high.

We got out to see if we could find the lockkeeper, but no one was there. Lunchtime.

Walking past the lock we saw the river far below, with no straightforward way down. Some three hundred yards downstream from the lockkeepers office, a girder bridge crossed the river on tall narrow supports, the roadway held high above the bank.

"I think it will be easier if we wait for the lockkeeper," I suggested pragmatically. It would be really awkward to get the kayak down there to launch."

"Okay," agreed Kristin readily, "Let us walk into town; buy some bread and take a lunch break."

We climbed the hill beneath an imposing chateau or defensive tower. But when we reached the bakery, open all morning, it had closed for the rest of the day. The other shops nearby had closed for lunch. Disappointed, but hardly surprised, we resigned ourselves to waiting till later to shop. Wandering back down the hill to our kayak, we scouted farther downstream in search of a place to launch.

Chateau at Castets-en-Dorthe.

20. Onto the River Garonne

Two or three days and nights went by; I reckon I might say they swum by, they slid along so quiet and smooth and lovely. Here is the way we put in the time. It was a monstrous big river down there— [23]

A long sloping path led down toward the road bridge, and under it to a slipway covered in fine, brown, dusty mud. The mud looked darker near the water, and closer examination confirmed our suspicions. More than a kayak length of the lower stretch was wet. The thin brown smear over the surface was as slick and treacherous as it appeared.

"Do you think we could manage to get afloat here without launching ourselves into the river before we are ready?" I asked.

"If we're careful. Maybe." We looked at each other. We could either wait or try it. We trudged back up the 350 yards to retrieve the kayak.

The trickiest part was the gradient of the slipway. The kayak on its wheels would drag freely down the hill if left by itself, and only the traction of our plastic clogs on the mud could prevent it escaping. Once we reached the wet mud, we would be out of control. With that in mind we should remove the wheels before we reached the wettest part, but that proved easier said than done. My feet were sliding long before we reached the slickest section.

Chocking the wheels to stop them rolling, we laid a seat pad beside the kayak and released the trolly straps. Then we carefully tipped the kayak onto its side on the pad, capsizing the wheels.

We still had a little farther to go, but this did not go according to plan. Clinging onto the kayak, we slid down the last few feet into the river, our shoes skating on the mud, momentum carrying us. The kayak abruptly afloat, we both lunged headfirst across it to avoid an otherwise inevitable ducking, balancing our head and shoulders over one side, our legs over the other. Swiveling around we dropped into our seats and sat, feet dangling over the sides, laughing at our escape.

"That was tricky! I conceded, rinsing the wheels in the tan-brown river. But as I did so, I saw how the current was whisking us away. We were already under trees, nearing a tangle of undergrowth.

"Quick! We have to get out from the shore!" Neither of us was ready, our muddy feet still out of the kayak, our two-part paddles in the cockpits not yet assembled. Fending off small branches we scooted forward into the middle of the river.

The urgency gone, we took a moment to clean the mud from our shoes, stow the wheels and fasten our spray decks. Looking upstream beyond the bridge, I could see how the massive Castets-en-Dorthe lock, beside the chateau tower, was already shrinking into the distance as the current carried us. Paddling or not, we were on our way downhill.

It felt good to be on a broad expanse of river, passing vineyards, chateaux, and old towns, cruising between hills. Nets hung from long poles at fishing stations above the river. We were cruising fast, yet the steep muddy banks that continued unbroken along each shore troubled me. At Castets slipway we had learned how tricky the mud could be, going downhill. Could we manhandle our heavy tandem kayak back up one of those slopes?

Canal meets Garonne River at Castets-en-Dorthe.

Here on the river we were entering the area that produces Bordeaux wines. On the right bank of the Garonne, onward toward Bordeaux, is the Entre-Deux-Mers region, producing the Premières Côtes de Bordeaux wines: a white wine appellation. On the left bank is the Graves subregion, producing reds, but also the sweet dessert wine, Sauternes.

Forty minutes from leaving Castets-en-Dorthe we passed Langon, and the spire of the thirteenth century Saint Gervais church. A dock inset into the shore, and a long quay and big crane, shows the place where parts for Airbus planes land after their voyage upriver from Bordeaux. Since 2004 the Airbus plant in the south of Toulouse has assembled the world's biggest passenger aircraft, the A380, capable of carrying 853 passengers. The major plane parts come from elsewhere: from Hamburg, Germany, from UK, and from Spain.

The biggest bits, the three sections of fuselage, two wings and the horizontal tailpiece, ship to France on three special roll-on roll-off ships. The upright tail fin flies from Cadiz, Spain, to Toulouse in a specially modified A380. It has a huge added cargo bay that opens above the lowered cockpit.

The roll-on, roll-off ships stop at Pauillac, the port of Bordeaux. The parts offload onto smaller vessels and barges to carry them upstream to here. The final 240km of their journey, from here to Toulouse, is on board flatbed trucks and trailers. Traveling at between 10 and 25km per hour, they use specially widened minor roads.

Having removed roadside obstructions, such as trees, to accommodate the width of the loads, Airbus, in compensation, replanted four times as many trees as they removed. The extra road width, when not used for transporting plane parts, accommodates special lanes for cycles and horses.

Although the route, known by the government as the *Itinéraire à Grand Gabarit*, bypasses most villages, one village remained on the route. The convoy of parts drives right through the middle of Lévignac, at night, with scant room to spare between buildings. Some parts are twenty-three feet wide and seventy-nine feet tall, not counting the truck bed.

As a sidenote, since our paddling trip, orders for the Airbus 380 have dried up. Airlines began to favor the versatility of a larger fleet of smaller planes. Fewer than three hundred of the massive planes sold, Emirates being the best customer. On 22nd June 2020, the last convoy delivered parts for assembly. The product line is due to close in mid-2021.

Seven miles on from Langon, on the right bank, is the town Cadillac. There, beside a house above a pontoon dock, we spotted a trailer loaded with whitewater racing kayaks. Drifting past, under a road bridge, we reached the outlet to a stream, Ruisseau de l'Euille. Three and a half miles up this stream stands the reason for this town's existence: the castle, Château de Benauge. Cadillac was the river port built to supply the castle. Jean de Grailly founded the fortified town in 1280, on behalf of the King of England. Much of the town wall still stands.

The seventeenth century man of title; the first Duke of Éperon, built his home in Cadillac. It was a magnificent Château on the outskirts of town. But despite such people of genuine title living here, Cadillac is better known in connection with a bogus title. It was one made up by someone born in 1658, more than eighty miles away, at Saint-Nicolas-de-la-Grave: Antoine Laumet.

It appears Laumet made up the title, *Antoine de Lamothe, écuyer, sieur de Cadillac,* which translates as something like Sir Antoine of Lamothe, squire of Cadillac. He claimed the title as if it were from the town of Cadillac.

Laumet became an explorer in North America, in New France which then extended from what is currently Eastern Canada to the Gulf coast of Louisiana. Far from home, he assumed his new name Cadillac, and phony title, designing a coat of arms to lend himself credibility. He registered his new coat of arms in Quebec, New France, claiming it as genuine, although as I understand it there is no record in France of any such French coat of arms.

Laumet seems to have lived a seesaw lifetime of fortunes and misfortunes. Sometimes he was honored, occasionally shut in the Bastille, once robbed by pirates. Placed in charge of projects, his conduct often saw him stripped of his duties.

Among his achievements, Laumet founded a trading post, Fort Pontchartrain du Détroit, in 1701. Relieved of his duties there, Laumet's next assignment was in Louisiana. However, the city of Detroit eventually grew up around the site of the trading post.

It seems that, to further his ends, Laumet assumed his false name and title to engender an illusion of grandeur, and his coat of arms to lend him credibility.

Two hundred years later, a spin-off of the Henry Ford Company, manufacturing automobiles, started a new brand. Its headquarters in 1902 was in Detroit. They named it Cadillac in honor of the founder of Fort Detroit, Antoine Laumet. They based the company logo on Laumet's fake coat of arms.

It is ironic how the name of such a sleepy town beside the Garonne should become synonymous with luxury American cars, known all over the world.

We needed provisions, yet as we swept past several towns, the shores looked too forbidding, steep, and muddy. So by the time we reached Langoiran beyond a bridge on the right bank, having come twenty miles downriver from Castets-en-Dorthe, Kristin had become insistent.

"We must stop to shop. If we wait for the perfect place to land, it will be too late, and everywhere will have shut. You might not care, but I want to eat tonight."

At a high, awkward, rocky shore, we swung the kayak around and ferry glided to land.

Loose boulders reinforced the lower part of the steep bank, above which was a band of concrete. A half dozen steps dropped through the concreted section, from steep grass above, to boulders below. A fence guarded the top.

Here seemed the best place to try to land, better than the mud banks elsewhere. While I clung to a slimy rock, Kristin found her canvas bag and the pochette, and scrambled onto the shore. As she began to climb, she slowed. The rocks were devilishly slippery, and she had to use her hands to balance. Higher up, the slope of grass concealed soft wet mud, into which she waded up to her calves in saturated goo. As she reached the top, I heard the animated voices of passersby greeting her. She stepped over the fence and out of my sight.

Kristin negotiates the mud at Langoiran.

I waited, clinging to the rock, trying to keep the bow of the kayak against the shore so the current would not catch it and spin me away. At the same time I tried to hold the hull away from the sharp rocks that would scratch at it. I considered getting out, but what would I do then? Stand holding the kayak or sit in the mud? The current was strong. If I tied and left the kayak, it would pendulum against the rocks.

Kristin was gone for a long time. I watched and counted the cars crossing the bridge. The traffic lights let twelve cars across at a time before changing, when, after a pause, twelve cars crossed in the other direction.

A dead fish joined me in my eddy, floating, pale, and bloated. I tried to get rid of it by pushing it out into the current. But each time, whisked away by the current, it regained the eddy downstream and drifted back to me. Then a dead rat, the size of a cat, joined in the circuit, and that smelled putrid. I tried even harder to get rid of that. I used my paddle to push it away but like the fish it kept returning. It was determined to stay.

I looked at the map. This afternoon on the river we had covered half of the distance to Bordeaux. Would we be able to find a place to land for the night?

Finally Kristin called down to me. She was at the top of the slope and starting back down. Sinking to her knees in the mud, she struggled forward, grimacing. She thrust her hands down to pull her shoes free, hauling up two big balls of clay, her red shoes embedded. She did not look happy.

When she reached the kayak, I took her bag on my lap under the spray deck while she cleaned up. Having scraped the mud from her shoes, she rinsed her legs and hands. With relief, I saw how easily the mud washed off leaving no stain.

When I alerted her to the fish, and the rat, lest she met them unexpectedly, she responded irritably, "Couldn't you have got rid of them?"

"So what happened?" I finally dared to ask when Kristin had restored her appearance, and her equanimity.

"You saw the mud? I was knee-deep in it by the time I reached the top. When I climbed over the fence to the sidewalk everyone just stared at me in horror! Then one man kindly took me around the back of a building and rinsed me off with a hose.

"I was worried I'd be too late for the shops. I found some shops nearby, including a bakery, but they had already closed. Someone told me of a supermarket at the edge of town, about half a mile away, and gave me directions, so I ran. Thankfully, it was still open. Did it seem as if I was away for a long time?"

"You took about an hour," I admitted. "I did wonder what was happening. I was afraid they would not allow you inside the shops, covered in mud. I felt sorry for you."

Back in the current, we sped along, mudbanks lining the shore. But a little more than a mile away, around the bend, we reached a floating pontoon and pulled alongside.

Small boats had moored there, and a group of people on the pontoon were trying to free a large log that had become wedged underneath. We asked if we could land, and after unloading the kayak, lifted it onto the pontoon. Then we clambered up the steep metal walkway to find a park: a field of short grass, some trees, and a public toilet.

Having confirmed that we could camp there, we carried up all we needed to set up the tent. The guardrails of the companionway were too close together for us to wheel the kayak up, but the men said we could leave it on the pontoon overnight.

They seemed worried, hurrying to fasten lines to the log, trying to at least secure it, having failed to drag it free.

"We have to move some boats," one explained, "they are not our boats, but they will be in danger if the mascaret moves the log."

"Is our kayak okay where it is, or would you like us to move it?"

"It's fine, safe. Just leave it!" It looked secure enough perched on the narrow pontoon as the sun sank across the horizon, reddening the few small clouds, the reflections blazing up from the quiet waters of the river.

The kayak, secure on the floating dock at sunset.

Nets dangling above the river mud, in morning fog.

21. Mascaret

A (tidal) bore is the hydraulic analogue of a sonic boom: a moving wall of water that carries the tide up some rivers that empty into the sea. For several hours after it passes the river flows upstream. [24]

I knew what mascara was. I had no idea what a mascaret was, but since everyone on the pontoon was busy, I left them to it and returned to Kristin at the tent. A little later I became aware of a rumbling sound, and then rushing like a strong wind through trees.

"What on earth is that noise?" I asked. "It's not an earthquake, is it?"

"Here?" asked Kristin. "I doubt it." We followed the sound down toward the river in the dimness of dusk to see what was happening. We felt no wind, but the dark river was rushing powerfully upstream, forcing a bow wave around the pontoon, and creating vortices and turbulent surges. It reminded me of the tidal rapids of the Swellies in Wales, or, in Washington, USA, the Tacoma Narrows or Deception Pass.

Finally I realized what all the French boaters had been concerned about when they warned us of the currents on the river. I had been naïve to shrug off their concerns like that. Sure, Kristin and I had kayaked in currents before. We had both kayaked down the Grand Canyon and played in plenty of tide races on the ocean. But water rushing this fast would have carried us helpless back upriver, had we been afloat.

Back at the tent we feasted on salmon, with endive, opening a bottle of Margaux wine by lamplight.

Later, Olivier, one of the men from the dock, came to invite us for coffee on board his boat, one of the little boats at the pontoon. Olivier, in jeans, was an ex-merchant marine from Bordeaux. He had shoulder-length, slightly greying, black hair tied loosely back, over a charcoal, long-sleeved, collared shirt. He wore a long, tangled beard, and a robust moustache, and spoke quickly in French. He had traveled the south Pacific and owned a ketch he intended to sail to South America. Meanwhile he lives on board the little boat we saw here.

In a faded green collared t-shirt, his thin companion, Francois, who wore a tormented expression under a short tangle of white hair and a pale facial stubble, spoke some English. He described how he had visited Ireland and Canada, and the United States. He said the USA deported him in the end for having the wrong visa.

When I asked about the mascaret, he explained, "It is a tidal bore. Surfers often ride the leading waves as far upstream as Cadillac, nine miles upstream from here. The tide reaches well beyond that, at least to Castets-en-Dorthe."

I had heard about tidal bores before. Kayakers surf the one that climbs the River Severn in Britain, but I had not known of any bore here. We had been lucky not to meet it.

Olivier, learning of our plans, told us of a pontoon in Bordeaux, on the right bank, where we could stop to visit the city. "I can give you the combination for the lock. It is not a place to camp," he explained, "but you can leave your kayak safely if you go into the city.

"If you need somewhere to camp, you will find another pontoon farther downstream. There is a fence there with a gate at the top too. The owner might leave the gate unlocked in the day, otherwise you will have to ask at the boat business. You could camp in the small field just above the companionway, but you have to get through the gate."

When we left his boat to walk back to the tent, the stars were dense and brilliant, the moon orange.

By morning, fog enveloped us. In the early half-light, we watched the shadowy shapes of trees gradually materialize far across the broad river. Slowly, as fog turned to mist, it progressively shrank down to the water.

Peeking upriver I saw, in the pastel pre-sunrise light, the perfect inverted image of the slightly misty trees in the river. A layer of haze separated the upright from the reflection.

Cone-shaped dip-nets hung limp, and damp, like morning spider webs, above the gleaming mud shore. The air held its breath. Every gurgle, and every bird call, sounded crisp and loud.

The river flowed sleepily past until, at 8.15, its direction changed abruptly, the water surging upstream. But despite the tide rushing so fast, it would take some time to completely cover the mudbanks. We should relax. There was no point in leaving before the tide slackened. Meanwhile, we began recharging our camera batteries on the pontoon, and, as soon as the sun burned through, we moved our dew-sagged tent from the shade to dry.

Around us stood rows of vines, heavy with bunches of blue grapes waiting for harvest. An isolated round tower, with a bell-shaped cap, stood among the vines. As the mist cleared, we saw the town beyond the field. Steps climbed a wall or bulwark from the vineyard to a château, and to the left of the wall, a row of houses marked the base of the hill.

Vineyards leading to Portets.

When Olivier came up to chat, we brewed espresso for him while he told us of the next spring tides. On the fourth and fifth of October, he assured us, the tide will cover the campground, and the mascaret wave will be big enough for surfers to ride. "Then it will run at ten knots" he explained. "It will be crowded with surfers!"

"That tower," he pointed to the one rising from the sea of vines, "used to be a toll booth. Passing boats stopped to pay the toll. The water once reached as far as that wall below the Château." He pointed across the vineyard to where the hill began. The river was now 350 yards from the hill.

Having strolled along the gravel road to the foot of the town, we learned more from an information sign. The 1736 Château, called Château Portets, or Château de Mongenan, is on the site of the Roman port, Portets, of 1,000 BC. Its well-manicured grounds began at the level of the top of the stone wall we could see from the river.

Whereas I had imagined the river then occupying all the flat land, that was not the case. A stream at the base of the steps from the chateau terrace once fed a channel, which widened as it ran toward the river. It passed the tower now in the vineyard. That channel, dug deeper and wider, was the harbor, although it appears from the sketch map that there was a second one adjacent.

Rowboats paid a fee for entering and mooring at the quay. They paid another toll for loading or unloading at the harbor. The pay booth was in the tower, called the Casco Tower.

When the Baron de Gasq built the château, he began work creating botanical gardens. His inspiration came from his friend, Jean-Jacques Rousseau, and from the ideas of the Swedish botanist, Linnaeus.

These gardens are notable, even now, for both their flowers and vegetables. Kept much as they were in the eighteenth century, gardeners here still grow the same varieties of vegetables, and fruit trees.

We made our way up the hill, through the old town, along narrow streets. The sidewalks, as usual, were little more than wide kerbs bordering the stone buildings. Shutters shielded the open windows or hung ajar.

Near the church, we reached an open market. Although starting to pack up for the day, the market offered fresh groceries, and meat and fish were for sale at a stall sheltered beneath an awning. We found Agen prunes again, and could not resist buying juicy figs, which just arrived from Spain. We also selected olives.

Back at the pontoon, as the tide slackened toward high, a small barge carrying cranes motored up and began to fasten chains around the jammed log. Olivier was busy freeing the lines that had secured the log overnight. Metal grabs on long arms wrestled the trunk. The barge reversed, trying to drag the log free, but found it firmly stuck.

It turned out the tree had twin trunks. The awkward V-shape had hooked around an upright metal pole that held the pontoon. Each of the trunks was about twenty-five feet long, yet despite its size, one had hidden beneath the pontoon. Only after the tide turned was it possible to haul the tree out. The barge operator then dragged the timber to the shore and lifted it onto the mud. His job complete, he motored away.

The excitement at the pontoon over, our way was clear to carry our baggage to the kayak, load, and prepare to leave. Olivier and Francois wished us bon voyage.

Disentangling log from floating pontoon, Portets.

Approaching pont de pierre, Bordeaux.

Pont de pierre, Bordeaux.

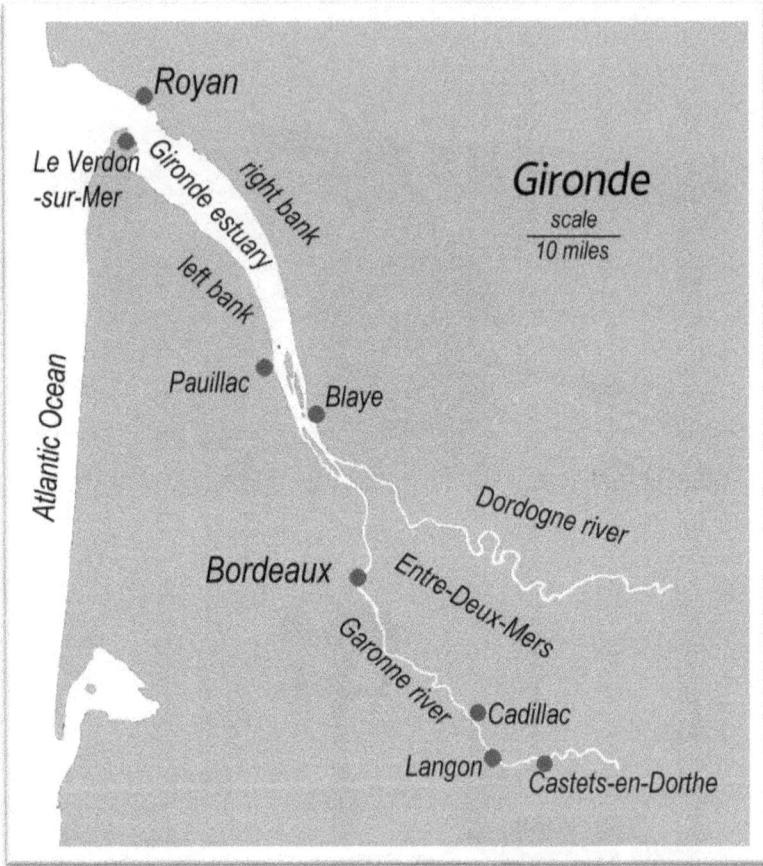

MAP 5. Gironde.

22. Bordeaux

...But on the Shores of Time,
Each leaves some trace of its passage.
Though each succeeding wave
Washes it out from the sand. [25]

Carried by the current, we passed châteaux and mansions. Little huts perched high above the bank, each like a wooden harvestman arachnid on its long spindly legs. A large, round, dip net hung out beyond each platform, dangling idly in the air. We were speeding toward Bordeaux, the pearl of Aquitaine. Yet neither its architectural heritage nor its renowned as a wine capital was first to bring Bordeaux to my awareness. No, it was something far less glamorous.

When I was at college, fiercely interested to read anything relating to kayaks, I came across the 1955 book: *Cockleshell Heroes,* by C.E. Lucas Phillips. It relates the story of Operation Frankton, a British commando raid on Bordeaux harbor, in 1942, when France was under Nazi occupation.

The Operation Frankton team trained in the south of England. A submarine was to drop them offshore of the Gironde estuary, from where they planned to paddle tandem kayaks all the way to Bordeaux.

Rigid kayaks would have been impossible to load onto the submarine, and the commonly available folding kayaks would take too long to assemble on deck once the submarine had surfaced. Instead they designed collapsible kayaks that could flatten.

These canvas kayaks were shorter, and wider, than ours, being sixteen feet long, twenty-eight and a half inches wide. Plywood reinforced the hull underneath for durability for dragging. Each weighed ninety pounds. Flattening from eleven and a quarter inches deep and folding inward, each formed a package just six inches thick. Folded, each would just fit through the twenty-one-inch diameter torpedo tube, to load on board the submarine. Brought out onto the submarine deck, the package could quickly clamp back into full kayak shape.

The ship assigned to drop them off was the HMS Tuna (N94). The 1936, T-class, Group One, diesel submarine was under the command of Lt. R.P. Raikes of the Royal Navy.

Once on the submarine deck, the team must pack everything, including explosives, carefully into each kayak before launching. But how to launch a heavy kayak and get the men safely aboard from the deck of a submarine? The easiest way would be to lower each kayak using a derrick, but like other vessels of its class, HMS Tuna had no derricks.

The ship's deck armaments, however, did include a four-inch gun. A metal girder strapped to the barrel extended it enough to use as a derrick. Each kayak in turn, ready loaded and manned, and hanging in cradles, swiveled out over the water. With the kayak lowered, the team pushed free.

The timing for the raid was in the winter of 1942, around the time of the new moon. The intention was to avoid any detection under moonlight. Incidentally, a new moon would bring spring tides, heralding the strongest tidal streams and the biggest range.

The submarine drop was about ten miles from the entrance to the Gironde estuary, on the night of 7th December. The approach was difficult because of the presence of Allied mines in the area.

Of the planned flotilla of six tandem kayaks, only five left the submarine. The skin of the sixth tore, on its way out through the torpedo tube.

Although an alarm sounded on shore, and searchlights turned on, the men were not overly concerned. Their kayaks would be unseen at that range.

The kayaks made their way toward the sandbanks that guard the entrance to the Gironde, where strong currents pour over the shallows. In the dark they must negotiate the tide races, and breakers, where the current squeezes through the narrows, and across the bars.

Not everyone made it through the rough water that winter night. One kayak vanished in the first tide race. A second kayak capsized in a later tide race. Attempting unsuccessfully to bail the swamped craft, the current swept them toward the lights of the Point de Grave lighthouse. Fearing for their mission, the remaining kayakers scuttled the swamped kayak and tried to tow the two men closer to shore.

The current swept them into the mouth of the Gironde, but toward the jetty at Verdon, at the south side of the entrance, where naval ships moored just offshore. From there, the two thoroughly chilled men had to swim the rest of the way to shore.

Just three kayaks remained, and it was already three in the morning. The six men, by bringing the swimmers closer to shore, had put themselves in an awkward position close to the jetty. How could they avoid the ships? The current was too strong to detour out around them. Somehow, they must pass close by, unseen.

They decided to drift past, one kayak at a time, keeping their distance. Maintaining a low profile, first one, then the next successfully passed. Those two kayaks regrouped, but they saw no sign of the third. What had happened? Left waiting, the remaining four men knew they must make haste if they were to find a suitable place to hide before the coming daylight.

In the end those two kayaks continued upriver, unaware of the fate of the third. In fact, the other kayak team had managed to slip past the ships unnoticed but passed the other kayaks in the dark. They made their way upriver alone.

Since reading Phillips's book, I had been aware of the Gironde estuary and Garonne River. The story had lurked in the back of my mind as a chronological geography. I visualized the terrain from the direction of the Atlantic, progressing inland, rather than from the direction we now traveled, but my recollection of the story rekindled my curiosity.

"I should like to see the Bordeaux docks," I confessed to Kristin, "and the U-boat pens. Bordeaux was the target of the Cockleshell heroes raid in the Second World War. The last part of our trip from here on down will follow their kayaking route in reverse, approximately."

"Really?" Kristin sounded incredulous. How could anyone not show interest and excitement?

But I at once recognized her scorn when she continued; "Bordeaux has such amazing historic architecture, and you want to spend your time visiting a submarine pen? I'd prefer to visit the Basilica Saint-Michel, for example."

Of course, I wanted to see it all, yet we would only be here for a few hours. Of all the sights to see in Bordeaux, I conceded, the submarine pens would surely be the ugliest. "I'm sure we'll come back sometime," I suggested hopefully.

Ahead was a railway girder bridge, constructed under the management of the twenty-six-year-old Gustave Eiffel, in 1860. Eiffel later became better known for the Eiffel Tower. The bridge, sometimes called the Eiffel Bridge, commonly went by the name: *la passerelle*, the footbridge, because of its corridors for pedestrians.

The Eiffel Bridge only recently became a historic monument, saving it from destruction. But although the river span is still there, demolition crews had already removed the access, for trains and pedestrians, before the bridge received its historic monument status.

A new, bigger, bridge under construction in 2006 now runs adjacent, carrying all the rail traffic. We swept under both railway bridges, water churning around the bridge piers, and then passed under the road bridge, Pont-Saint-Jean. Then we saw, a hundred and fifty yards ahead, the famous pont de pierre. Its stone-edged, brick, bridge arches repeated elegantly across the river, decorated at intervals above with ornamental lamp standards. On the left bank, pointing up from above the closer buildings, stood the slender gothic spire of the basilica Saint-Michel.

"Wow!" I could not help expressing my wonder. And then, "That is a beautiful bridge! So many arches! How many are there?" They were difficult to count from the kayak.

Napoléon Bonaparte ordered the building of the pont de pierre, *stone bridge,* to enable him to move his troops rapidly. At that time, a ferry was the only way to cross at Bordeaux. By design, or by coincidence, the bridge, built between 1819 and 1822, has the same number of arches as the letters in the name Napoléon Bonaparte, which add up to seventeen.

The pontoon, where Olivier suggested we should stop, extended from the right bank before we reached the bridge. Its metal deck trembled in place against the current, held by massive, grey-painted, cylindrical uprights. We spun to face the current and ferry glided to the pontoon, where we clung on tightly lest the turbulent yellow brown current wrenched us away. The current was so powerful, I felt ill at ease until we had hauled the kayak from the water. Even then, I felt safer wearing my flotation vest on the pontoon while eating lunch. The river rumbled noisily, churning past the supports in wheeling, caramel, vortices, and bursting upward in huge boils.

Kristin agreed to humor me in my quest to see the docks. We tested the gate lock combination to ensure we could return if we both left, before stepping into the street.

There, I experienced a culture shock: joining a stream of city pedestrians. I felt out of place, enveloped by the crowd of crisply dressed men in collared shirts, and skinny businesswomen in tight jeans and heels. Scruffy or not, we were at large in the city.

A tram-ride across the pont de pierre carried us between the stately terraced buildings that lined the left bank. It skirted past the spectacular church building Kristin would have preferred to explore.

World War II U-boat pens, Bordeaux.

We disembarked near our destination and were soon walking across broad quays, each a web of scraffito patterns: embedded railway lines running everywhere.

The U-boat pens, a stark fort, stood reflected in the glassy-green water of the inner harbor. The hangar openings, like deep square eyes, glowered from beneath a massive concrete roof more than thirty feet thick. These pens could withstand bomb attacks.

The escalating arms race in the Second World War would eventually lead to bombs capable of penetrating even such heavily reinforced concrete armor. Nevertheless, Hitler rightly considered Bordeaux safe from Allied bombing raids. He counted on the human shield effect. Any air attack would be certain to result in heavy civilian casualties.

Heavily fortified pen number 6.

Leaving the submarine pen basin, we followed the water's edge, past the narrows, to the outer basin, and another third-of-a-mile toward the lock. Deep-hulled, wooden, fishing boats lay on the hard, or stood shored up for maintenance, the weathered wood grain as gnarled and furrowed as tree bark. Old girder cranes stood idle, some short, compact, and boxy. One, reaching tall and slender, stood poised like a giraffe about to step forward. Along the edge of the quay, massive cast metal bollards waited for heavy hawsers.

Wooden boat under repair.

Beyond the lock gates, upstream, is where, for centuries, vessels have chosen to dock. There on the outside of the river bend, the current keeps the channel scoured deep. This is where, in December 1942, a row of supply ships stood under guard against the quay.

I imagined the place where we stood as it might have been then at night, a hive of activity. I imagined cargo loading and unloading, submarines sneaking in through the lock for refitting. Here would have been rail traffic, dark cars and trucks, armed guards, and searchlights.

On December 10th, 1942, two kayaks spent the last day of their journey hidden in tall reeds, on the left shore. That was opposite Bassens, no more than two miles from here. That night, the fuses having been set on the mines, the kayaks separated for the raid, one to follow each bank.

The leader, Hasler, with his teammate Sparks, explored this side as far as here. Skirting wide to avoid the lights that illuminated the water around the lock entrance, they crept up to the ships moored just upstream and placed limpet mines on several of them.

Meanwhile, the other kayak team scouted the far shore, finding no ships. Returning, they mined the two ships at Bassens they had watched from their daytime hiding place.

Their mission complete, the two kayaks met again in the dark and retreated some twenty miles downstream to Blaye. There they separated before landing. Independently, each pair tried to escape.

It is now known that the kayak team that vanished in the dark on the first night, when the group passed the ships at Le Verdon one at a time, almost made it to Bordeaux too. Unfortunately, when their hull ripped against something sharp in the dark, their kayak sank, and the men swam to shore. They had reached Isle Cazeau, near the confluence of the Garonne and Dordogne, a dozen miles from their target.

Overland, Hasler and Sparks headed north to Ruffec, looped east to Lyon, and then south to Marseille. They thought no one would expect them to take such an indirect escape route. Now skirting the Gulf of Lion to Perpignan, they crossed the Pyrenees into Catalonia. From Barcelona they traveled inland to Madrid and onward to Gibraltar.

They both reached England again after several months. Without the help of the French Resistance, it is probable they would have eventually met the same fate as all the other team members who reached land. The Germans captured them, tortured some, and shot them all.

The submarine that had dropped them off, HMS Tuna, was one of just six of the original fifteen, Group One, T-class, submarines to survive the war. In September 1945, it was placed on reserve and beached on the mud at Falmouth, England.

As we looked out from beside the lock, we could see construction in progress in the river: four enormous bridge stanchions, two each side of a central shipping channel. These were for a new bridge that will meet land just 150 yards from here. It will be the Jacques Chaban-Delmas Bridge, a vertical lift bridge.

Due to open in 2013, it promises to be the largest lift bridge in Europe. To allow ships to pass, the whole central span will raise. A counterweight inside each of four hollow corner pillars will drop vertically, lifting the span to a height of 175 feet (53 meters).

The bridge will carry four normal traffic lanes plus two bus lanes. A separate, extra, outer lane each side will carry pedestrians or cycles. The lift will have an area equivalent to a football pitch. Had work on it already finished; we would have found it the shorter route back to our kayak.

23. A Night in the City

She's coming in
On a wing and a prayer, [26]
One wing at a time,
under pont de pierre.

We were anxious to reach our proposed camping spot before the owner locked the gate, and before the tide changed direction. Catching the tram back through the city, I gawped at the architecture we passed, feeling guilty for having denied Kristin her opportunity. Bordeaux is a magnificent city.

Dismounting at the square on the right bank by the pont de pierre, we stopped for espressos and croissants. We also bought some local wine, for the evening, before letting ourselves through the gate onto the pontoon.

It would be just one-and-a-quarter miles downstream to our destination. As we sped under the pont de pierre, we spotted a long, dark blue, ship approaching the bridge from the other side, on the outside of the bend. It moved slowly against the current, and when I looked more closely, I recognized its cargo as a single, massive, airplane wing. On the ship's navy-blue hull, painted in bold white letters, were the words: *Airbus A380 on board*. This was one of the ships that carried airbus parts to Langon.

Since the load was flat, it would be able to pass under the low bridge, something the larger plane parts barely manage. When transporting the largest pieces, even at low tide, it can be necessary to partially submerge the barge to get sufficient clearance.

Aircraft wing on route to Toulouse.

We were soon around the bend to the next pontoon where a few, small, immaculately varnished, wood strip, recreational motorboats had moored. There, Kristin quickly ran up the companionway to the gate, to where a man was preparing to lock up. He kindly asked inside the building to see if it would be okay for us to camp, and then waited while we lifted the DoubleShot onto the pontoon and grabbed what we needed. As he secured the gate after us, he mentioned it would be someone else who would unlock it in the morning.

"You can't go down at night," he warned.

I wanted to be sure it would be open in the morning.

"Of course," he assured me, but no, he did not know at what time.

We surveyed our campground, a small rectangle of rough ground covered in short dry grass between patches of brambles. A hedgerow of trees blocked the view of the river behind us, while an earth rampart, about three feet high. bordered the rough access road paralleling the river. At the far side of the lot, a cement-block boundary wall blazed under garish graffiti. Beside us, beyond a fence, a neat two storey wooden house overlooked the river. Immediately behind the house, beside the road, stood a single storey workshop.

Sailboards leaned against the workshop, where a neat stack of timber stood. On the side fence hung a painted sign depicting a group of people racing past in a speedboat, smiling, water-skis on board. The sign advertised lessons for boat licenses, with phone numbers in Verdon and nearby Lormont.

I walked onto the street to see the front of the building where, mounted on the wall, a tidy cutout depicted the side elevation of a sporty, wood strip, motor-launch. It revealed the workshop's purpose. Chantier Nicolas was a boatbuilding workshop, specializing in the restoration of vintage, inter-war and post-war, motorboats such as Chris-Craft, and the boats of several classy Italian builders. The neat wooden fence and wooden buildings were right in character.

I looked down at the uneven road under my feet. Laid with heavy, square, cobbles, grass grew from the cracks. Beyond the far kerb, lurking in the grass like a snake, lay a railway line, obstructed by small, old, wooden open boats that leaned from their keels toward the road. I scanned in both directions along the road and saw minor factory units or warehouses, each individual plot separated by low ramparts of bare earth and weeds.

We chose a place in the field on which to camp. The ground was uneven, with vegetation so roughly mown that a stubble of bramble and thick stems stood stiffly, all brightened by pink pea vetch. We gingerly pruned the prickly bits and set up our tent as the light faded.

In darkness, standing looking through the metal pontoon gate that barred us from the river, we could see the golden lights of the city, its spires illuminated. Reflections of the city lights shapeshifted and distorted, rippling and shaking in the black of the turbulent river. I loved the way the reflections shimmered, but I saw how the lights made the surrounding darkness deeper.

"Would you be able to spot a passing kayak in the dark," I wondered?

"I doubt it," Kristin admitted, "even if I specifically watched for one." With no mandatory blackout in Bordeaux during the war, the night view from here in 1942 would have been just like this. Beautiful.

It rained later in the night, a somehow reassuring rattle against the cocoon of our nylon tent. It created an irrational feeling of security, as if it were safer to sleep soundly when it rained.

Awake early to wet grass, we watched the sky brighten until ten o'clock. With no sign of anyone to unlock the gate, we left the tent standing in the hope it might dry. Walking past the small factories and workshops we returned to the pont de pierre.

I felt at ease. The tide would continue to flood for some time before it slackened and turned. Too early for us to leave, we had time to dally. Time to relax outside a café nursing a coffee, and then to find a supermarket. Tempted by the fatty aromas, we bought a hot takeaway meal of half a rotisserie chicken with fried potatoes. We devoured it eagerly, back at the tent, with the customary drop of wine.

One hundred and fifty yards from our camp, across the road in the opposite direction from our first exploration, lay two large stone structures. These solid blocks, constructed of pale stone, and rectangular in shape, each stood thirty feet wide and about as high, and one hundred feet long. Surprisingly inconspicuous, despite their substantial bulk, these buildings were oddly windowless and doorless.

A Night in the City

Unravelling the puzzle, we found that these were to have been the supports for a bridge to cross the river here. Work on the bridge began in 1910 but was never completed.

The bridge was a transporter bridge, having girder towers more than three hundred feet tall, (95 meters). The planned structure had a girder gantry high above the river. A platform, suspended from the gantry, would ferry traffic back and forth across the river, just above the water.

When necessary, the platform could lift to the gantry, well out of reach of tall ships. Hanging above the current, it was better than a ferry, while free of the constrains of a low bridge.

At the time, two other such bridges were already in operation in France, one at Marseille, and an older one at Rouen. Completed, it would have been the biggest of its kind in the world.

Bridge construction halted during the First World War. Afterwards, resources were insufficient for the project to restart. The city demolished the two massive girder towers, already erected, during the Second World War, to prevent invading forces from using them. These two, large, incongruous blocks, the last remnants of the project, are a strange monument to what might have been.

Once the tide turned, and the gate to the pontoon had opened, we were ready to leave. We slipped quietly mid-stream, past the barges and cranes constructing the huge bulwarks that will support the new bridge. Temporary docks, which extended from each shore to make the construction work easier, routed us along the middle.

Past the mouth of the lock that we visited yesterday, the river curved, until the industrial landscape of Bassens came into view, framed beneath the tall Aquitaine suspension bridge. This bridge, completed in 1967, relieved the burden from the pont de pierre. It is the last bridge before the Atlantic, still sixty miles away.

The Bassens docks followed: a dry dock, and a coal yard. Grain from a row of tall dusty silos poured onto a ship via a conveyor: a moving feast attended by hundreds of pigeons.

Bassens grain silos.

In 1942, somewhere within the overgrown shore opposite Bassens, the two commando teams hid with their kayaks in the reed beds all day before their last night afloat. They felt secure peeking out to watch all the activity across the river, over here.

Bassens docks felt familiar to me in a coastal way. Most commercial docks I have seen by kayak have been on or by the coast. Yet although we were already in the tidal zone, we had not yet reached the official estuary, the Gironde.

Out of the corner of my eye, I spotted a tall, modern, sailboat sweeping past, motoring stealthily at speed. Its low profile, dark metal-grey hull and superstructure, and dark mast and rigging, gave it a sinister, almost military, appearance. It blended into the background, camouflaging so well it caught my attention only by its movement, despite its size.

24. Wine

*"I can certainly see that you know your wine.
Most of the guests who stay here wouldn't know
the difference between Bordeaux and claret."*[27]

Many small areas, individually lauded for their wine, make up the wine growing region known as Bordeaux. We had passed some of these on our way to Bordeaux on leaving the canal at Castets.

Bordeaux wines grapes grow on the *left bank*: the left bank of the Garonne and the Gironde estuary, and *right bank*: the right bank of the Dordogne and the Gironde estuary. Between the Garonne and the Dordogne is a triangle of land known as *Entre-Deux-Mers*. This translates directly as *between two seas*, but derives from *between two tides*, *deux marées*: the tidal reaches of the Dordogne and Garonne.

North of Bordeaux, and west of the Garonne and Gironde, stretches a north-pointing peninsula. It is a broad wedge of land, twenty-five miles wide at Bordeaux, narrowing for over fifty miles to the point where the Gironde estuary meets the Atlantic. Along the eastern strip of this peninsula, the left bank of Garonne and Gironde, lies the Médoc region. Physically the land, loosely described, is gravel overlaid by small pockets of limestone and clay.

Most Médoc wines come from north of Bordeaux, on the left bank, although other wines such as Graves, and Sauternes, come from upstream beside the Garonne, just south of Bordeaux. Cabernet sauvignon blends predominate.

Even though gravels tend to drain well, much of the area was swampy marshland until drained, and reclaimed, by Dutch engineers. That was as recently as the seventeenth century, contemporary with the construction of the Canal du Midi.

That might seem long ago, but much of the wine production on the left bank is historically recent. It was seventeen hundred years earlier when the geographer Strabo reported back to Rome that the Bordeaux area had no wine production. That prompted moves to remedy the situation right away, for Strabo's observations were timely.

That is because, following the Roman conquest of Britain in the first century AD, the Romans needed wine to provision the garrisons stationed there. This staple initially shipped from Italy, around the Iberian Peninsula, in ceramic amphorae. If wine could ship from the Gironde to Britain instead, voyages would be safer. Ships could cut four thousand miles off each round trip.

It made perfect sense to plant vines here by the Gironde, especially on the drier right bank where the land is predominantly of limestone and clay. Those wines have continued to find a market. Ever since those days of Roman occupation, Britain has obtained wine from Bordeaux.

The Gironde right bank produces model Merlot-based blends. Saint-Émilion, and Pomerol offer well known examples.

When pressed, grapes, even red ones, produce clear liquid. Fermenting this liquid will produce white wine. Wines from Entre-Deux-Mers are primarily white wines, blending three grape varieties: principally sauvignon blanc, with Sémillon and Muscadelle.

Wine

Sauternes, from the left bank of the Garonne, uses the same grape varieties, but affected by noble rot, a grey mold that afflicts the grapes there. The mold imparts a special raisin flavor to the sweet wine.

The tannins, and red color, come from crushing grapes, and fermenting everything, including skins: *macerating* them, for a couple of weeks.

From the twelfth to fifteenth centuries, Aquitaine was under the rule of English kings. Then, the most common wine shipped from here to Britain was a dark rosé, known in France as *clairet*. By macerating for only a few days before straining out the solids, the result was a fruity, light red or dark rosé wine, low in tannins.

At that time, clairet came mostly from Graves, on the left bank of the Garonne between Castets and Bordeaux. The name, *claret* in English, has referred to Bordeaux wines sold in Britain ever since. At first applied to those dark rosé wines, *claret* is since used to describe the dark, dry, purplish reds, rich in tannins acquired by macerating for a longer time.

Whereas the early clarets were perfect for drinking soon after production, showing no improvement if kept longer, the later, more tannic ones, can improve in the bottle. They can mellow, and generate complexity, for up to twenty years.

Wine was so important to Romans, they transported vast amounts. Yet shipping wine requires robust containers. Although the Romans did transport wine in clay amphorae, the vessels most associated with their wine storage, amphorae can be fragile and do not travel as well as wooden barrels.

The Romans learned from the Gauls to make use of the oak forests they found in France, making barrels to transport wine back to Rome. At their destination, the wine storage was in amphorae. But the effect of the oak, on the flavor of wine held for a time in barrels, did not go unnoticed. Wine makers still use oak. Some flavor the wine in the original way, by keeping their wine in oak barrels for a time, while others soak oak staves in their wine. Either method adds extra tones of complexity to the wines, imparting tannins, and vanillin.

Even if Bordeaux wines from the left bank have a shorter history of production than some on the right bank, they do not lack for reputation. Some of France's most widely recognized wines come from here, such as Margaux, Pauillac, Saint-Estèphe, and Saint-Julien. In addition, many smaller and lesser-known wineries also produce top quality wine. Cabernet sauvignon blends of the left bank are the reference for Cabs worldwide.

Expensive Bordeaux wines sold for investment, to be aged and traded over time, can cost hundreds of dollars per bottle when first on the market. When the wine is at its prime for drinking, fifteen to twenty-five years later, some fetch double, triple, or quadruple their original price.

But those only make up about three percent of the annual production, and Bordeaux accounts for about a quarter of all wine made in France. That leaves a lot more Bordeaux wine available at more palatable prices, and most wine originating here has the reputation of being reliably good.

On our trip we chose to buy inexpensive wines, from vineyards situated as close to where we stopped as possible. Wine was not the primary focus of our trip. We could easily have made it so, given more time. But we did sample Languedoc wines while on the Canal du Midi. Having arrived in the Bordeaux region, we now savored the classic, dry, Cabernet Sauvignon blends this region is known for: what I, as an Englishman, call claret.

25. The Gironde

*...the ebbing tide had gone out three-quarters of
a mile, and to get to the river the canoes had to
traverse this bleak expanse of sandy mud.*[28]

The Gironde estuary begins where the river Dordogne approaches
from the right to meet the Garonne. The rivers converge, leaving
a narrow point of land at the end of five miles of chemical plants
and oil storage silos.

"It's a big junction!" I reminded Kristin. "It might be
bouncy!" Where the two rivers enter the Gironde was a major
milestone for us, and it proved a turbulent meeting place for the
powerful currents too. The surface bulged and swirled, twisting
the kayak this way and that, as it swept us downstream.

A string of islands divides the river downstream of the
confluence, long, narrow, pointy islands, low, vegetated and
easily flooded. The first, the more than seven-miles-long Isle
Cazeau Cantenac, extends its southernmost tip into the River
Garonne. By choosing to experience the meeting of the rivers,
rather than follow the narrower western channel, we missed any
view of a string of villages famed for their wine chateaux.

One mile beyond the end of Isle Cazeau lies the small Isle
Paté. This island lies offshore the town of Blaye, which has been
a port for at least two thousand years, and long fortified. But in

1685, just three or four years after the Canal du Midi opened, King Louis XIV ordered new defenses built to protect Bordeaux from the Atlantic side.

The renowned French military engineer, Vauban, directed the project, building three structures. He constructed a citadel at Blaye, a defensive fort in the form of a round tower on Paté Island, and a fort across the river: Fort Médoc.

The extensive Blaye citadel encloses the remains of the medieval castle and basilica, which stood on a rocky outcrop overlooking the river. At my first glance, I saw the cliff ahead, not realizing the extent of the military additions that blend in.

Fort Médoc proved the only contentious construction. The land on that side was low-lying and marshy. The sediments, even at depth, proved too soft for a foundation to support a stone fort. So, Vauban ordered a low structure, digging ditches and raising earth ramparts. It had barracks for three hundred men.

Fort Médoc was not situated in the healthiest place. The marshes increased the incidence of insect-spread diseases. Of 1,200 soldiers tasked with the construction, in just one day one hundred went to hospital, ill. Because of the dampness of the ground, each soldier was issued with three planks of wood, each plank eight inches wide and six feet long, for use as a bed. Each soldier also had a bale of straw, on which to sleep.

We sped past, the tide falling fast, watching mudbanks and boulders appear all along the shore. I began to wonder if we would find any easy landing at low tide, for I had no map of this part of the waterway of any practical use to me for planning.

The next major fortification we approached, nine miles farther on, looked more fort-like than the citadel at Blaye. What I thought were low buildings, seen from a distance, loomed high as we drew nearer. Buoys marked out an area of deep water around massive docking structures in front of the gaunt, windowless, concrete edifices.

The Gironde

This stronghold is more recent; commissioned from 1981 to 1983. Unlike Blaye, which was built to protect those inside, these massive defenses protect the people outside, from what hides inside. This was a working nuclear power station.

France generates upward of seventy percent of its electricity from its fifty to sixty nuclear power stations. That is a higher percentage of total electrical power produced by nuclear fission than in any other country. United States, as the biggest overall producer of nuclear power, generates less than twenty percent of its total electricity in that way.

Here, the Blayais plant has four pressurized water reactors. In December 1999, a combination of intense winds and a high tide caused flooding, breaching the sea walls. Water flooded part of the plant, sparking electrical failures. As a result, two of the four reactors shut down, in what became a level 2 International Nuclear Event.

Afterwards the sea defenses, once repaired, were more than ten feet taller, and more strongly reinforced. This added layer of defense, serving like the extra ring wall at Carcassonne, will hopefully be sufficient to fend off the next attack.

At the turn of the low tide we followed an avenue of channel markers toward the shore. A rectangular dock sat on a mudbank, stranded several feet above the water. At high tide it must float offshore, its long sloping companionway then reaching from the dock to land above water instead of mud. We had no way to reach the dock except by wading up the giant pillow of mud.

We passed by, entering a narrow channel. Looking between the mudbanks into a little harbor, we saw how much the low tide had drained that area too. The pontoons lay high and dry, parallel to the straight ribbon of water. The fishing boats, and sailboats, tied against them also sat out of the water on the exposed mud. Gleaming silkily, the mud was soft, fine, saturated. It swallowed my paddle blade without resistance when I probed.

Gradually the tide covered the mud.

Eager to land, I found the pontoon tantalizingly out of reach from where we floated at the edge of the mud. Wondering what to do, I saw how the tide was flooding, the edge of water creeping slowly, but inexorably, up the mudbank.

"If we are patient, we can avoid wading through the mud," I pointed out, hoping Kristin would agree. "Are you warm enough to wait?"

It felt decidedly draughty on that little strip of water. Immobile, I began to feel the chill edge of the breeze. But the chill was relative, just a late summer chill. Beneath my float vest I chose to wear just t-shirt and shorts. It made me once again pity the men of Operation Frankton, paddling at night across waters of December temperatures. They had to find a place to land in the dark before dawn. Creeping ashore at high tide, their first concern was to find somewhere to hide their kayak, where they would rest motionless, throughout the day.

The Gironde

Upon evening darkness, they had to drag their kayaks through mud, like that beside me, to reach the water at low tide. Setting off again, they must have remained muddy, dealing with the cold all night, while trying to avoid detection.

Inch by inch we floated closer until, crouching, and stretching, I stepped across to the sloping pontoon. Tying off the bow line, I helped Kristin ashore, leaving the kayak afloat, now out of reach.

It felt like a winters day at the seaside as we hastened to scout the area. "Look!" I pointed out happily. "A bar-grill. We can get a hot meal!" But to our disappointment, when we looked closer, the grill had closed for the season.

Picnic tables stood on a grassy area just a few yards from the grill, near to public toilets. Here seemed an ideal place to set up the tent beneath a tree.

There was nobody around on this side of the harbor. Across the water, new sidewalks and a resurfaced road ran past a building under construction. But even there, nobody was visible. Everywhere seemed deserted.

As soon as the tide allowed us to float the kayak up to the dock, we unloaded and lifted it, mud-smeared, onto the pontoon. Already in darkness before we were set up, we ate at a picnic table by flashlight.

Considering where we were, I saw no reason why we should not make it to Royan tomorrow, given reasonable weather. So far, conditions had been benign.

After a comfortable night on flat ground, we crawled from the tent to find clear skies, a golden glow preceding the sunrise. Birds sang while we made espressos, at breakfast, at the picnic table. The day could not have seemed more promising.

Calling Richard on the phone, we told him of our progress. He offered to meet us at Royan, at ten next morning.

"Make sure you are waiting, packed and ready to go, "he added. "It will be Camilla's birthday tomorrow, and we are having a party, so I can't be late."

We had a date! But we had to reach Royan first, another thirty miles. We impatiently watched the water; eager to leave yet disinclined to fight an incoming tide.

"The tide should turn today between ten and midday," a passing angler replied to Kristin's query. That would be an hour earlier than yesterday at Bordeaux. He also revealed our location, Collanges, pointing out that it did not appear on our map. He left us and, walking toward the sea wall, found a position to work his rod and line at the farthest corner.

Waiting for the ebb tide at Collanges.

26. Where are we?

*"That map maybe alright enough," said one of
the party, "if you know whereabouts in it we are
now."[29]*

Across the estuary lay the famed left bank Médoc Bordeaux wine
growing region. On this side, the town of Cognac is situated inland
about thirty-five miles east of Royan. Distillation of Cognac liquor
takes place in the region around Cognac, a development from the
winemaking that began in Roman times. However, it was the
Dutch, trading salt and wine from Cognac, who began "burning"
wine of low alcohol content. The distillation made it last longer
on voyages. Seafarers could dilute it into something resembling
wine. In Dutch, burned wine is *brandwijn,* hence brandy.

Distillers refined the single distillation process, to use a
double distillation, in the seventeenth century, when Cognac first
appeared. Of course, the drinkability improved when kept for a
little longer in the oak casks used for transport. People began to
enjoy drinking it without added water. From then on, Cognac
became associated with brandy.

Cognac, as a brandy, has not been in production for as long as
Armagnac, recorded as early as 1310. However, since Cognac is
more widely available, it is better known.

201

Kayak across France

While we waited, we dried our clothes, damp from the splash of waves yesterday, and scooped water to rinse our muddy paddles and kayak. As we worked, we watched a fisherman, in a small open motorboat, turn from the estuary into the harbor entrance. Dressed in a navy-blue sweater and flat cap, he stood motionless, hands thrust in the pockets of his canvas trousers, steadying the tiller between his legs. The harbor was coming to life.

Feeling a breeze in our favor, we left after the tide had slackened, yet before it turned. I felt joyful, moving again, speeding across the muddy expanse of water. The Gironde here was three miles across, but it would widen to six-and-a-half miles, before pinching into a neck, three miles wide. We would pass through that final throat, where we could expect the fastest currents and tide races, before reaching Royan.

Fishing huts, Gironde estuary.

Skimming along close to the shore, we passed many long, narrow, wooden jetties standing far above the water, each sporting a small crane and a hanging basket-net. These nets were square, unlike those farther upstream which had been round. Periodically, another narrow channel cut inland into the low plain. Some were simply drainage from the marshes, but many led into little harbors sheltering small fishing boats, and yachts, at pontoons like the one we had used last night.

Gradually, from our high tide vantage point, we could see over the low shore toward higher limestone hills, and farms. We passed salt marshes, where hunters hides were visible. On the drier patches, a few cows grazed. The landscape was open and bleak. Across the water, in the distance, we could make out the shadowy shapes of girder cranes.

We had become accustomed to the cloudy-green, sometimes grey-green, color of the canals, and then to the yellow brown of the water in the Garonne. Even in Bordeaux the river was opaque, a rich caramel color on account of all the clay and silt it carried. Gradually, it began turning yellow, and eventually it started to clear toward a translucent green. The water here was more saline. The salt binds the suspended particles, encouraging them to sink, gradually clearing the water. The progression was very noticeable as the afternoon brought us closer to the ocean.

Then we reached white limestone cliffs. They looked just like the chalk cliffs along the south coast of England, where I grew up. It felt to me as if we had reached the sea, yet we had not.

Kristin called out. She pointed to a small cylindrical stone tower, up on a ledge near the top of the cliff. "Look," she said, "Near the tower, there are windows in the cliff face."

Sure enough, all around the tower were holes cut into the rock. They might once have been military defenses, but nothing looked forbidding.

Soon, what appeared to be a fortress came into view. It stood at the edge of the rounded end of the cliff, the latter faced in stone like the base of a castle tower. A stone wall flanked the building, raising the natural defensive height of the cliff alongside. Yet, despite resembling a fortification, this was a church.

Somber, like the nuclear power station earlier, it appeared devoid of windows. At least that is how it looked until we drew close and could see more clearly. But even so, I spotted few windows.

This was the église Sainte-Radegonde, built in 1094. The outcrop was an ideal site for the bastide, built around the church: the village of Talmont-sur-Gironde. Founded in 1284, by order of Edward I of England, the village fills the entire small outcrop. Fortifications enclose the clifftop all around.

A stream that runs along the base of the eastern side of the cliff, allows a narrow access into a small harbor. We stopped paddling and drifted, while waves slapped the kayak and broke across the rocks along the shore. In the brief time we paused, the current and wind carried us past.

Despite the tempting opportunity to land here, to explore the village, I decided against. I had read of the church on its clifftop perch but was unsure how far it was from Royan. The village was not on my map.

From here, a long bay curved to end at a promontory about two miles distant. Across from that, we could see how the left bank pinched in, narrowing the estuary. Was that the entrance to the Gironde? Was it already Royan we could see at the far end of the bay? Somehow, I did not think we had paddled for long enough.

My book on the French canals, now stowed away somewhere inside the kayak, included a page-sized street map of Royan, showing the marina at the western end of a beach. It showed how a promontory protected it from the west, but the map scale was too large to show more than the main part of the town. From that information, we could be looking at Royan.

Where are we?

We pressed on, soon reaching the town at the promontory, and there was the marina!

"That was quick!" commented Kristin. "The tide must have helped us a lot!"

"And the wind too," I agreed, but then I began to have doubts.

"The town seems too small," I decided. "The marina too. The map in the book suggested that both the marina, and the town, were quite large. This does not seem to be much of a town. I don't think this is Royan."

Thinking it over for a few minutes, I convinced myself we had not arrived yet. Foolishly, I felt confident enough to urge Kristin on, without stopping to check.

We sped around the corner to see the cliffs pocked by doorways and windows. There were carved terraces and caves dug into the cliff all over the face, at multi-levels, for houses and a hotel. Wooden platforms extended out to the familiar fishing huts with dangling nets.

Here we had entered a tide race: a tidal rapid that rushed us along, the water jumping and crashing, soaking us as we sped briskly past the cliffs. Fascinated by the cliff dwellings, and drawn to look up, I could feel the leap and crash, and the twist of the kayak beneath me.

After about two miles, we reached a beach when, looking back, we could see how houses covered the hill we had passed. Had I been wrong to assume the town we had passed was too small to be Royan? The street plan had not shown the topography. The hill might hide much of the town from view, from upstream.

"What if that was Royan?" Kristin asked, still unconvinced by my earlier confidence. "We will paddle farther and farther away looking for it. We should stop and ask someone where we are."

We were drifting fast, and I was tempted to keep going to see what lay around the next corner."

"No," Kristin insisted. "Pull in here. I'll go and ask those people by the sailboats."

A row of small catamarans stood high up on the beach, sails of pastel blue, and green, flapping freely in the breeze. An instructor was addressing a class of children, all clad in lifejackets. Reluctantly, I spun the kayak around. We ran ashore onto the sand before the current could carry us beyond the beach.

Once we had hauled the kayak far enough from the waves, Kristin ran up the beach, leaving me standing with my back to the wind. I watched as she approached the group. Everyone closed in around her. Someone pointed an arm back the way we had come, but that meant nothing to me.

But when Kristin made her way back down the sand to join me, she announced that we were at Royan beach, and had in fact passed the marina.

"He says the marina is back there."

The tide was running so strongly it seemed futile to try to fight both current, and wind, to get back. We should wait for the current to slacken. We walked the beach to find shelter from the wind, beside the cliff, and found fossils in the rocks. As we watched the tide rips at each end of the beach, we dug our feet into the sun-warmed sand.

"The end of a trip doesn't always turn out quite how you expect it to, does it?" I murmured, recalling my first French canal trip.

***

Tim and I had four weeks available when we began that trip. It took us three weeks, to paddle just halfway across France. It seemed obvious we would have to head home from somewhere along the way, never reaching the Mediterranean. But then, and only because the Saône and the Rhône were in flood, we completed the second half in the remaining week. We flew downhill. I could not believe how fast we traveled in those last few days.

Moving fast. River Saône in spate.

But the devil is in the detail. Our whole trip had been on an impulse. Our busy schedules beforehand had led to sketchy planning, but we were confident we would be able to figure things out day by day. Now we had reached the Mediterranean at Port-Saint-Louis-du-Rhône, how would we get home in time for work?

Tim Franklin portaging a barrage on the River Rhône.

"We'll catch a train back. The kayak can go in the guard's van," Tim confidently asserted. In UK, we knew, bicycles and other awkward baggage could always travel in the open space of the guard's van, watched over by the guard. We assumed it would be the same here. But we discovered Port-Saint-Louis-du-Rhône had only a freight line. The nearest passenger line would be at Marseille, fifty miles across Provence. That was too far away. We had no time left to paddle there.

"We can catch a bus to Marseille. You know, I'm almost certain the buses here have roof racks," said Tim. "We can put the kayak on the roof."

I thought it unlikely but went along with him as far as finding out where the bus would stop, and when. The schedule promised a bus in the morning, but the service was infrequent.

Next morning, we were up and ready as quickly as possible. Accustomed to loading our kayak, and how long that took, we now found it awkward to organize everything to carry home. Too slow, we missed the bus. We stood forlorn beside our mound of stuff, at the roadside.

"We may as well try to hitch a ride while we're here" said Tim, sticking out his thumb. "Perhaps we'll get picked up by a truck." No such luck.

We were not standing there for long before an orange Citroen 2CV came beetling along the road, from the opposite direction. It braked, did a little wiggle on the road, and then sped past. Ten minutes later it returned and pulled up. The young woman at the wheel was a kayaker and she laughed at our story. She laughed at the sight of us, and she laughed again at the improbability of hitchhiking with an eighteen-foot-long kayak.

Yet she helped us tie the kayak onto her flimsy roof rack, its bars no thicker than a finger and separated by no more than three feet. She fed us into the back of the car onto an unpadded seat, a canvas sheet across metal bars, and passed in our bags of gear. She had buried us before she slammed the doors. The remaining gear filled the front passenger seat.

"Marseille? I will drive you to the railway station!" She announced cheerfully."

I squirmed in my seat under my baggage. The familiar stench of our fetid socks, not having dried for a month, was troublingly powerful, despite the window flap hanging open. I peered from behind my bag, trying to see the countryside as we sped across Provence, passing the Étang de Berre, an area of ancient wetlands and lagoons on the Rhône delta. All-too-soon we were in the ancient city, Marseille, outside the railway station. Our bags lay in a heap beside the red kayak. We waved our heartfelt thanks as the little orange car sped away.

At Marseille railway station in1979.

"Non! It is too long," said the man at the ticket office, shaking his head.

"Let's try another," said Tim solemnly as we walked away disappointed. We tried several. Eventually we were successful, buying a one-way ticket for a single passenger with accompanied baggage. I would discover how that could go astray later. In the meantime, we did not have enough money left for a second passenger ticket. Even that did not dampen Tim's spirits.

"Well, that worked out okay, didn't it?" He laughed. We had figured out how to get the kayak back, and we could return it to Kirton Kayaks later. But there was still an awkward detail to settle. One of us would have to hitch-hike today.

"Toss for it!" Tim said, producing a coin and spinning it into the air. "Quick! Heads or tails?"

27 Why do it the easy way?

...join they all together
Like so many clouds consulting for foul weather[30]

We waited impatiently at Royan Beach as the afternoon slipped away. A sign on the beach warned, in red letters, in both French and English, "Danger Violent Stream". I could see the current. A roiling eddy line lashed out from the rocks we had passed. The water pushed out in a wide curve. Closer to shore, water circled back in the opposite direction as an eddy toward the rocks. Here, the surface was choppy with steep little waves rasped up by the wind against the current.

The leaping and tangling interface between these flows, the eddy line, showed in two colors. Close to shore, in the eddy, sand filled the water, camel colored and cloudy. That water was shallow. The eddy line marked an edge. Beyond, where the current had scoured deep, the water rushed past blue green.

Looking across the channel, I could make out cranes, and a tower, if a little indistinctly. They looked about four miles away. From where we stood, the cliff blocked our view of where the left bank must end.

The tidal range can be about thirty feet here at spring tides, and the falling tide had left our kayak high and dry. When the current eventually slowed, the eddy lines by the shore began to weaken. The vortices spinning along the eddy lines became shallower, less vigorous.

We carried our kayak back to the water and launched into the eddy, cruising easily until we hit the main current by the rocks. There we were almost halted. Even sprinting against the current we made scant progress.

"I thought it would have slackened off more by now," called Kristin over her shoulder.

"Me too!" I replied, "but it's the wind too. Those cliffs are focusing it against us."

Heading back.

Little by little, we forged forward. Kristin suffered most of the spray from the bow, but as she lifted her blade at the end of each stroke, water sprayed back at my face. It tasted salty. In anticipation I closed my eyes each time, opening again to the fresh sting of salt behind my sunglasses. Now I had time to view the cliff dwellings more clearly as we crawled past. Some tunneled into the rock, others stood, built on rock ledges. The rock, creamy yellow, I thought was limestone, but may have been sandstone.

The sea-carved caves offered natural shelter for prehistoric people, the first to occupy them. By the Middle Ages, enlarged, they afforded a convenient base for pirates and wreckers. From here, the outlaws could spot the distant ships as they approached the estuary on their way to Bordeaux. By the time the ships entered the estuary, the pirates could be ready to intercept them. With Aquitaine under English rule, it was not until the sixteenth century that heavily armed troop ships, disguised as merchant vessels, put an end to the piracy.

It took a vigorous push to recover the distance of little more than a mile back to the marina. The view had changed. It was difficult to see any way into the marina, between the mudbanks exposed by the falling tide. With our paddles gripping the mud beneath mere inches of water, we scooted slowly along the shallows to the harbor. There, boats lay aground on a bed of greasy mud, their mooring lines limply tethering to the similarly grounded pontoons.

Ahead was a closed lock, to an inner harbor where boats could remain afloat, but that would only be accessible when the tide was high. A slipway ran down from the quay, but the clay-slick ramp ended abruptly, stopping a few yards short of the water. Those few yards of mudbank were discouraging. If we were to wade through the mud to the ramp, we would still have a challenging time clambering up without slipping. Yet the ramp offered the only feasible way to get the kayak out.

"Well," I congratulated Kristin, "We made it! But it is not going to be much fun getting ashore! I think we'll have to wait until the tide rises enough to bring the kayak out." I frowned. "That could take hours."

"If you want to wait here," Kristin offered, "I think I should see if I can book a night in a hotel before it gets too late." But the way to the slipway looked too treacherous. There were ladders, although to reach them she would first have to climb the mud. Did we have any alternative?

"Maybe that ladder over there," Kristin pointed to a corroded metal ladder fixed to the quay on the other side. Slime green near the bottom, bulging with rust blisters, and holed in places, its broken end hung above the mud.

"It is closer to the water than the others," she pointed out. "If you can hold the kayak close enough, I might be able to reach it if I stand up."

With Kristin gone, I drifted aimlessly. The bow, now light on the water, caught the wind, turning me. The eddying breeze blew me slowly across the shrinking pool to the far mud, held me there for a moment and then pushed me away again.

A silky white egret drifted down and landed nearby, with steely beak and legs. I watched the breeze ruffle its long feathers as it stalked the mud looking for food. Not so long ago, as recently as the early 1990s, egrets were rarely, if ever, seen in France. Yet they had once been common. They featured in the paintings on the ceiling beams at Capestang.

Egret populations were all but eradicated in the eighteenth and nineteenth centuries; slaughtered for their plumage to decorate fashionable hats. Leading up to World War I, feather merchants and processors employed more than twenty-two thousand workers full time in London alone. Paris had its own sizable hub.

Why do it the easy way?

Egret, Meschers-sur-Gironde.

In 1912, when the Titanic sank, fine plumes were the most valuable class of merchandise on board. Insurance claims for the forty cases lost totaled 3.2 million dollars, in today's currency.

It is hardly surprising that egrets vanished from France and were absent for a long time. But toward the end of the twentieth century they began to return. Now they breed in France again and overwinter in their thousands.

Recalling the fifteenth century depictions of egrets, at Capestang, took me back, scanning over our whole trip from Sète, through Béziers, Carcassonne, Toulouse, and Bordeaux, to finish here. This multifaceted journey was not ending how I had expected. How could something so straightforward become so messy? If I had heeded Kristin's suggestion when we first arrived here, we could have landed easily on the slipway and would already be celebrating the completion of our trip.

When Kristin returned, peering over the edge above the ladder and calling my name, her voice sounded uncertain.

"I managed to book a room," she said, "but I discovered from the receipt that we are not at Royan. We are at a place called Meschers-sur-Gironde. You really wanted to finish at Royan didn't you? We could stop here instead if you like. Or should I take the key back and cancel the room?"

I had set my sights on Royan. We were within reach, too close to the finish to choose to stop short.

"I'll be as quick as I can!" Kristin called before she hurried away again.

When she returned, she was breathless from running. As she scrambled down the metal ladder again, she said the receptionist had told her it was twelve kilometers to Royan from here, seven or eight miles.

At six-thirty we slipped out from the mudbanks, into the splash of wind-whipped waves, and pointed ourselves northwest to pass the cave dwellings on the cliffs for the third time.

I looked around me. Conditions had changed. The wind had freshened and veered around to the southwest. The tide, now slack, no longer helped us. Out in the Gironde, a ship had already swung around on its anchor chain to face the start of the new flood. We must get a move on.

28. Royan

"Oh Oysters," said the Carpenter,
You've had a pleasant run!
Shall we be trotting home again?"
But answer came there none
And this was scarcely odd, because
They'd eaten every one.[31]

The wind whipped up the waves as we pushed hard to make as much distance as possible before the tide grew too strong against us. Once again, we passed the beach; Royan Beach as the sailing instructor had called it. Beyond lay more rocky points and small beaches. Across the water to our left, I could now see the tip of land that marked the western end of the Gironde, where the Frankton team had struggled through tide races as they headed from the submarine into the estuary.

The wind continued to veer. It came now from the west, picking up by the minute. I heard the first rattle of rain as much as I felt it. Then, rounding a prominent headland, I could see what lay ahead. A long low beach stretched to the next promontory. The tip of a more distant cliff peeked out from behind that. Pinpricks of light already speckled each dark point.

The clouded sky hastened the growing darkness. Through the motion of the kayak, I could feel a change here in the waves too.

The wind-blown chop was running hard, and short, like a rapid heartbeat across the estuary, but through it came the slower, breathing, heave of the Atlantic.

The waves, already breaking over our kayak, filled our spray decks. We had chosen lightweight ones to seal the cockpits for the canal trip. They had been comfortable, and adequate, all the way until now. Here, as water pooled heavily on my lap, sprayed in around my legs under the elastic, and poured in at my waist, I wished I had something sturdier.

"Nigel!" Kristin's urgent cry came at a violent lurch. A wave had broken hard against us, jolting the kayak sideways.

"It's getting rougher!" she added more calmly. "Should I edge and use my paddle to brace when a wave breaks like that, or just keep paddling? I'm more used to handling a single kayak."

"Just edge into the waves. We can brace together if we get a big breaker." Truthfully, I never imagined we would be out in any waves like this.

The full-on rain hit in a squall, ripping across the water. "Oh no!" I groaned loudly at the elements. "Not yet! Not now. Couldn't you have waited?" The deluge piled on one more layer of discomfort.

We forged forward, at a snail's pace now, toward the flecks of light smudged by the rain. As night closed in, the distance gradually narrowed. Through the darkness and the curtaining rain, I could pick out the marina wall, like a shadow against the hill, but no sign of an entrance. We made for where I expected to find it.

I caught the rain-shrouded flash of navigation buoys, and closer, I spotted the almost invisible shape of a sailboat. Running alongside the harbor wall toward shore, its green starboard light gleamed.

"The entrance must be nearer to the beach than I expected," I alerted Kristin, as I changed our course. "Unless that sailboat has got it all wrong. It rather looks as if it is about to land on the beach."

I was glad when we reached the harbor wall. We sneaked right up close before turning toward shore. As each surging swell piled against the wall, it lifted and shoved us forward, speeding us along. Surf rolled in the bay just a few yards ahead, revealing where, at this state of tide, the water shallowed toward the beach.

I suddenly saw the port and starboard entrance lights high above us on the stonework. A moment later we spun around the end of the mole into the marina entrance. Ahead stood a mass of rain-slashed masts, rocking in the dark, rigging whistling. We had found the small boat harbor, the pleasure-boat marina, our haven in the night.

We may have finally found the correct Royan, but we still needed somewhere to land. The rattling sailboats clustered tightly as if everyone had come here for shelter. Fogged portholes gleamed yellow. We poked around pontoon after pontoon, exploring the dark watery passages between, but could find nowhere big enough for us to land our kayak. If we could not find somewhere here, we would have to resort to landing on the beach, through the surf. I wanted somewhere easier.

I was becoming discouraged when we found an empty space at a pontoon, near the boundary fence, at the very back of the marina, by some tour boats. Wearily, we hauled the kayak from the water for the last time. Rain crackled loudly against the metal all around.

I gave Kristin a hug, rainwater running down our faces, then, "Let's check the gate up there." A companionway led up to the tall fence bordering the marina, where we found the gate unlocked, but only from the inside. If we both left, we would be unable to return. As we clomped back down the slope, we agreed to first gather our bags into the partial shelter beneath the companionway. We set to, intending to completely empty the kayak.

"What would you like to do tonight, Kristin? It is about nine o'clock already. We can't stay in here, and if we go out, we have to take everything, including the kayak."

"I doubt we can camp around here. Setting up in such rain would be hideous anyway. One of us should go to look for a hotel."

"What about the gear?"

"Well, let's gather everything together at the top of the walkway first, and then carry the kayak. We can prop open the gate to take everything out in one go."

"We could padlock the kayak to the outside of the fence for the night. There is no point in taking it any farther tonight. It'll be challenging enough with everything else."

"I'd consider getting a taxi to carry our stuff," suggested Kristin. "I could call one from the hotel. Otherwise it'll take us all night."

We had a plan. Saturated and cold, we wasted no time.

We were busy gathering loose items into our bigger blue IKEA bags when the gate opened. Someone came striding down the companionway, their feet clanging heavily on the metal. Aware that we had no permission to be here, I fussed over my bags, expecting a reprimand. The man stopped and stood tall over me as I crouched, the rain pelting.

"Hello, did you come from Bordeaux yesterday?"

"Yes, why?"

"My friend saw you on the Garonne, from a sailboat, a big one, dark grey."

We had seen it pass, the big, stealth, racing yacht, under power.

He continued, "I work at the point between the Garonne and the Dordogne, I watched for you to pass. I wondered where you were going. Where will you stay tonight?"

"We are going to look for a hotel."

"Are you sure? You may stay on my yacht if you prefer," he offered. "It is really close, just a few meters away." Such a wonderful offer, we could not refuse.

Gathering our stuff, we wheeled the kayak closer, stashed some of our things inside again, and carried what we needed on board. The beautifully crafted, wood-paneled, interior revealed three small cabins.

"Make yourselves at home," he encouraged, offering us the cabin in the bow. Then, he lent us his passkey and gave us tokens for the shower in the marina building, suggesting we hurried to a Tiki restaurant along the beach first.

"You might still be able to get served a meal if you are quick. You can shower on your way back."

Soon we sat at a table, pouring Graves wine into two glasses, a hot meal on its way. Beside us, our change of dry clothes waited in waterproof bags, for after a hot shower.

Back at the boat, our host, Angel Martinez, said he sailed whenever the opportunity arose. Tonight was Friday night, so he had come after work to prepare. If the weather was right, he looked forward to sailing all weekend. "I hope you will be cozy in your cabin," he smiled.

When we stepped into the galley next morning, after a comfortable sleep, we discovered Angel had been out to buy breakfast and coffee for us.

He came with us to show the way when we wheeled the kayak up the companionway and out of the marina.

"These parking places are for the marina," he waved an arm dismissively at the parked cars. "You need a pass to get in here," he explained, as he led us farther along the marina road to the first public parking area outside.

"Here," he said, "this is where you should wait for Richard." He left us there and went back to prepare for his day.

The morning was clear, but the breeze rattled the rigging against the masts of the sailboats in the marina and whistled through the stays. The air smelled of the ocean. A carousel stood beside the road, its crown-like double decker structure a reminder we were at a seaside town. But the carousel was idle. The holiday season was over.

All the fun of the fair.

"So," I said to Kristin, giving her a high-five, "we made it from sea to sea, from the Mediterranean to the Atlantic! You and me! Well, with the help of plenty of people along the way."

Richard sped into the parking lot, looking left and right, bang on time at ten in the morning. Full of energy and enthusiasm, he was happy to see us packed and ready. He reached back behind his seat for cups: the colorful ceramic Kri-Kri cups Kristin made in Seattle, and then a bottle of champagne. Popping the cork, he poured a toast to our success.

"I tried to keep it cold!" he said, his hand feeling the temperature before he poured. Then, suddenly serious, he cautioned, "We can't drink it all! Load everything first. Just down the road they have the best oysters!"

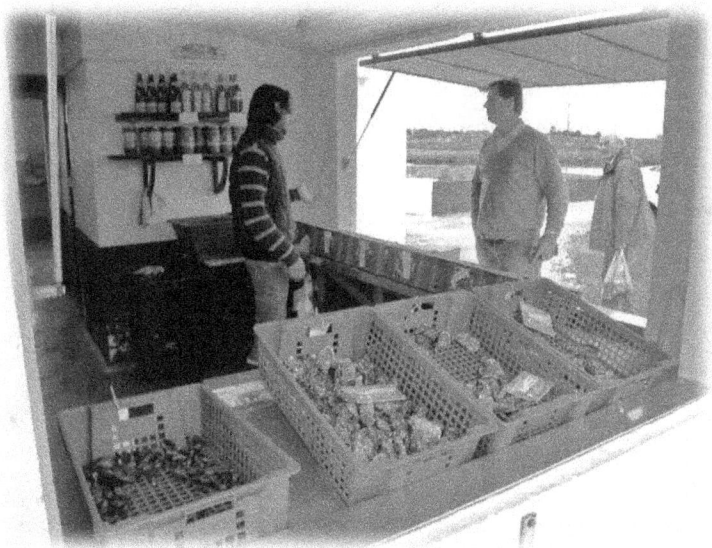

Richard selecting oysters.

At the tiny oyster shack, we sat together on a white-painted cement wall beside two ceramic oyster plates. On each plate was an artful arrangement of a dozen succulent oysters, on the half shell; oysters of two kinds. What a wonderful finale. We had begun our trip at Sète, a place famous for oysters, to finish here, throwing empty shells into the marsh behind us as we sipped champagne.

Acknowledgements

Thanks to Richard Öhman of Point65 Sweden, for your wonderful logistical support, for loaning us the kayak, sourcing wheels when ours failed, and collecting us at the end. Your help throughout, in so many ways, made our trip not only possible, but more fun.

Tim Franklin, your creative plan for our great trip together from the English Channel to the Mediterranean in 1979, was the inspiration for this later one. So, double thanks! I hope I did not malign you too much in relating aspects of our trip together. *The rain falls upon the just and the unjust feller, but mostly on the just because the unjust has the just's umbrella.*[32] I forever wonder how the spin of your coin fell to my favor. I took the train!

Starting from the beginning, thanks Patrick and Martine, of Sète, kayakmed.com, for hosting us, guiding us around Sète, and launching us on our way.

For help on route, my thanks to the following: the happy French group: Pascal, Chantal, Jacky and Nanou. The English couple: Marilyn and Trevor. Jean Pierre and Bettie of *Patte Blue*.

Of the special lockkeepers we met, Jean Louis and Frederika, for the wonderful evening after fishing Kristin out from the canal, and for letting us camp in your garden. And when wheels fail, and lockkeepers drop everything to come to the rescue: Luce, and Jacque.

Other lockkeepers? I hold profound respect for lockkeepers. They have the patience of saints. Their overall concern is safety, so they run a fine line between following the rule book and excising their own judgment. Thank you for being there!

Acknowledgements

Also thanks to Philippe Wielgus and his sons from north Agen. The lovely lady who helped us find a camp spot at Moissac. Olivier and Francois, at Portets. The owners of the Chantier Nicolas dock and field at Bordeaux. Angel Martinez at Royan for your generosity and hospitality toward two wet strangers, welcoming us overnight on your wonderful yacht.

On the canals and beside them, everyone offers a friendly greeting to voyagers. To those whose job it is to maintain the canals, and to those who welcome the strangers who use them, thank you. You make the world a better place.

In researching and authoring this book, I had invaluable help from the Los Angeles sommelier, Peter Nelson. Thank you for your wine-related advice.

Of course, thanks to Kristin Nelson. Quirky, creative, and bright, you made our trip fun, and made writing about it even more enjoyable. Once again, your proof-reading with constructive criticism helped improve this book.

Plate of oysters.

Did you enjoy this book?

You can help.

Each honest review helps to bring the books you like to the attention of other readers. If you enjoyed this book, I would be glad if you could spend a few minutes to leave a review, however short, on the book's Amazon page.

Thank you so much.

Some other titles by Nigel Foster:

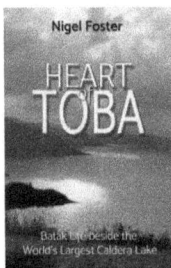

Heart of Toba. (*Nigel Kayaks*). A kayaking exploration of Batak Life beside the World's Largest Caldera Lake. An adventure to discover the hidden wonders that make life by Lake Toba, and on its volcanic resurgent island, Samosir, so special. (North Sumatra, Indonesia.)

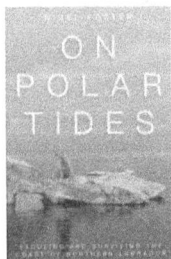

On Polar Tides. (Falcon). Paddling and surviving the wilderness coast of Northern Labrador. Ungava Bay and Labrador is the realm of polar bears, fierce mountain squalls and extreme tides. Woven into the account of two kayak journeys are tales of early exploration and plane wrecks. There are encounters with polar bears, and Inuit seal hunters. A German weather station stands on a remote island, installed by a submarine crew during the Second World War. All in this remote region where green auroras twist in the night sky, and fog drifts around stately icebergs.

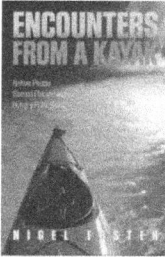

Encounters from a Kayak, (Falcon). Thirty-nine stories from Foster's diverse experiences around the world. Tales about what makes kayaking special. Arranged into four sections, the stories tell of Creatures, People, Places, and Flotsam and Jetsam. Color images throughout

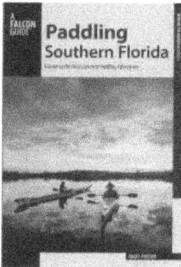

Paddling Southern Florida. (FalconGuides). An updated guidebook to more than fifty paddling trips in Southern Florida. Includes road access to launch and finish, detailed route guidance with points of interest, suggestions for accommodation, dining and rental options. Sidebars offer handy detail about Florida wildlife, weather and history. A must if you are to make the most of a trip to Florida. (FalconGuides)

The Art of Kayaking. (*Falcon*). All you need to know about paddling. From necessary skills to essential gear, this is the distilled work of Foster's innovative instructing, expeditions, and kayak design experience. Find sound advice for beginners, alternative techniques and subtleties for finesse and fine control for the advanced.

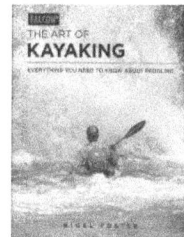

Color photo action sequences, maps, and diagrams, make this an easy-to-follow book for all levels from beginner to expert. On calm water or rough, there is something for everyone.

More at *www.nigelkayaks.com*

Bibliography

Bristow, Philip *Through the French Canals.* Navigator Publishing 1970, (plus many later editions).

Phillips, Lucas C.E. *Cockleshell Heroes: Epic Exploit of the War*, Wm. Heinemann Ltd. 1956.

Rolt, L.T.C. *From Sea to Sea.* Euromapping 1994.

Kurlansky, Mark. *Salt: A World History.* Penguin 2002.

Goubert, Pierre. translated by Steve Cox. *The Ancien Régime: French Society 1600-1780.* Harper and Row 1969.

Gast, René. *The Canal du Midi and navigable waterways from the Atlantic to the Mediterranean.* Editions Ouest-France 2009.

Hanson, Thor. *Feathers: the evolution of a natural miracle.* Basic Books 2011. (Ref: information chapter 26).

End Notes

----

[1] Nigel Foster.

[2] Robert Burns,1785.

[3] This, and other polar bear encounters, are described in Nigel Foster's book: *On Polar Tides, paddling and surviving the coast of Northern Labrador.* Published by Falcon 2016

[4] Paul Valéry. From the poem: *Lost Wine*.

[5] Lewis Carroll. From the poem: *The Walrus and the Carpenter*. From the book: *Through the Looking Glass*, 1871.

[6] William Shakespeare, from the play: *The Merry Wives of Windsor*. (1564-1616).

[7] W.H Davies. From the poem: *Leisure*. From the book: *Songs of Joy and Others*. A.C. Fifield, 1911.

[8] Nigel Foster.

[9] Nigel Foster.

[10] Mick Jackson. From the book: *The Underground Man*, Penguin, 1997. (p 25).

[11] Adapted from a nursery rhyme, first recorded in the sixteenth century.

[12] William Shakespeare. From the play: *Antony and Cleopatra*, Act II, Scene II. (1564-1616).

[13] Robert Frost. From the poem: *Wild Grapes*. First published in the December 1920 issue of Harper's Magazine.

[14] D.H. Lawrence. From the poem: *Mosquito*. 1920.

[15] Gustave Nadaud. From his 19th century poem: *Carcassonne*.

[16] Edwin Markham, 1852-1940 The poem: *Outwitted*. Published in *The Shoes Of Happiness: And Other Poems*. Doubleday, Page & Company, 1915.

[17] Kenneth Grahame, from the book: *The Wind in the Willows*. Methuen, 1908.

[18] Antoine de Saint-Exupéry. From the book: *Vol de Nuit*. (Night Flight). 1931.

[19] W.H Davies (1871-1940) From the poem: *Thunderstorms*.

[20] Geoffrey Chaucer. From the poem: *A Monk*.

[21] From the Irish folk song: *Moonshiner*, from circa 1900.

[22] Nigel Foster.

[23] Mark Twain, from the book: *Adventures of Huckleberry Finn*, Chatto and Windus, 1884.

[24] David K Lynch. From an article on *Tidal Bores*, Scientific American, 1982.

[25] Henry Wadsworth Longfellow.

[26] Line inspired by the 1943 song title by Harold Adamson.

[27] Basil Fawlty, from *Fawlty Towers*, the TV comedy.

[28] C.E. Lucas Phillips. From the book: *Cockleshell Heroes*, Heinemann, 1956. (p143).

[29] Jerome K Jerome. From the book: *Three Men in a Boat*. Dent, 1889. (p57).

[30] William Shakespeare. From the poem: *Venus and Adonis*.

[31] Lewis Carroll. From the poem: *The Walrus and the Carpenter*. From the book: *Through the Looking Glass*, 1871.

[32] Cormac McCarthy, 1835 1894.

www.ingramcontent.com/pod-product-compliance
Lightning Source LLC
Chambersburg PA
CBHW022006080426
42733CB00007B/496